The
Marshall Cavendish

International

WILDLIFE

ENCYCLOPEDIA

VOLUME 9
FLY – GOR

MARSHALL CAVENDISH
NEW YORK · LONDON · TORONTO · SYDNEY

Introduction by: Professor D.L. Aller
General Editors: Dr Maurice Burton and Robert Burton
Consultant Editor: Mark Lambert
Production: Brenda Glover
Design: Eric Rose
Editorial Director: Nicolas Wright

Revised Edition Published 1990

Published by Marshall Cavendish Corporation
147 West Merrick Road
Freeport, Long Island
N.Y. 11520

Managing Editor: Mark Dartford BA
Editor: Nigel Rodgers MA
Production: Robert Paulley BA
Design: Edward Pitcher

Printed and bound in Italy by LEGO Spa Vicenza

Library of Congress Cataloging-in-Publication Data

Marshall Cavendish International wildlife encyclopedia/general
    editors, Maurice Burton and Robert Burton.
        p. cm.
        ''Portions of this work have also been published as The
International wildlife encyclopedia, Encyclopedia of animal life and
Funk & Wagnalls wildlife encyclopedia.''
        Includes index.
        Contents: v. 9. FLY-GOR.
        ISBN 0-86307-734-X (set).
        ISBN 0-86307-769-2 (v. 9).
        1. Zoology–Collected works. I. Burton, Maurice, 1898-
II. Burton, Robert, 1941-   . III. Title: International wildlife
encyclopedia.
QL3.M35 1988
591'.03'21–dc 19

Volume 9

Flying lemur

There are 2 species of this living parachute, known as colugos or flying lemurs. Both are very alike and they have presented zoologists with a problem, for they have no close relatives. They are not related to lemurs, despite their name, and are placed in an order on their own between the insectivores (shrews, moles, hedgehogs) and the bats. Their teeth look superficially like those of the insectivores, they move about in the air like bats, and in face they look like some of the lemurs; but their teeth are unlike those of any other animal. Each of the incisors and canines has 2 roots and each of the lower incisors is comb-like, with 10—12 fine points.

One species is found only in the Philippines, the other is widespread through southeast Asia, from Burma to Borneo. It is cat-sized, 1½ ft long, with a tail nearly 1 ft long. It has a sharp muzzle and large eyes and there is a membrane of skin from the sides of the chin which continues in a broad web down either side of the body, taking in the forearm with all the fingers and the hindlegs and toes and going right up to the tip of the tail. The fur is a mottled grey, fawn and buff.

Peter Ward

Anticipation or retrospect? Watched intently by its baby, a female flying lemur licks her lips as she wanders through the foliage that forms the main part of her food.

Ace glider
Only one kind of mammal truly flies: the bat. Many mammals make gliding flights and of these the flying lemur is the best equipped for it. It lives in forests and rests on the branches of tall trees in a vertical position, its body and gliding membrane lying close to the bark and harmonizing almost perfectly with it. Usually it chooses a hollow in the tree. When disturbed it moves rapidly along the branch, perhaps making its rasping alarm call, climbs up the trunk and launches itself in a long smooth flying leap to the next tree, anything up to 150 yd away. The efficiency of its parachute is such that it loses less than 40 ft in that long glide. Arriving at the next tree, it runs up the trunk to gain height, ready for another takeoff should that be necessary. It rarely comes to the ground and should it do so it makes for the nearest tree at the gallop and uses its sharp, curved claws to shin quickly up it. While sailing through the air the outline of the spread membrane is almost oblong.

Floral meals
At dusk the flying lemur glides to a favourite tree and begins feeding on leaves, flowers and buds. It is said to eat fruit also, but one kept in captivity ate fruit only reluctantly. It pulls food towards its mouth with a front paw and bites off the leaves or flowers. Water is probably got from wet leaves.

Advanced offspring
Mating takes place in January to March and 60 days later the single baby—twins are rare--is born. The baby is 10 in. long at birth, ⅓ the length of the mother. She leaves it in a tree hollow when she goes foraging or carries it clinging to her teat or fur with its teeth, getting further support by grasping her fur with its clawed toes.

Rare or not rare?

For a long time zoologists believed the flying lemur to be rare, although the local peoples not only ate its flesh but used its fur to make hats. It was first discovered by Europeans in 1768 but it is only within the last 25 years that we have known it is common throughout southeast Asia—when somebody discovered how to look for it. It is commonplace among naturalists that someone who is experienced in looking for a particular animal can readily find it, whereas anyone else can look and look and find nothing. It is a case of 'getting one's eye in'. It was the same story with the sloth, looked upon as rare until a GI stationed in the Panama Zone during World War II spent his free time looking for sloths and found that they were very common.

Too often an animal is called rare simply because nobody has looked for it in the right way. There was the scientist who, before going to Madagascar, was asked by a colleague to try to bring back specimens of a very rare fly. On arrival in Madagascar he showed a drawing of the fly to the local people and offered a reward for every specimen they brought him. The following morning he was awakened early by noisy shouting, to find some Malagasy urging a cow towards his tent. The cow was swarming with flies—the rare fly!

class	**Mammalia**
order	**Dermoptera**
family	**Cynocephalidae**
genus & species	*Cynocephalus volans* *C. variegatus*

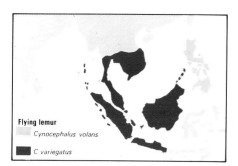

Flying lemur
Cynocephalus volans
■ *C. variegatus*

Flying phalanger

Sometimes called flying squirrels in Australia, because they look outwardly alike. Flying phalangers are, however, not even distantly related to squirrels but are true marsupials like kangaroos and possums.

There are five species distributed over the eastern half of Australia, one species overlapping in the south into Tasmania, and one species of sugar glider in New Guinea. They belong to three types: the pigmy or feathertail glider, the 3 species of sugar glider and the greater glider. The first is mouse-sized, just over 6 in. long, of which a half is tail, olive-brown above, white below. The sugar gliders are nearly 16 in. long, of which one half is bushy tail, with a fine silky fur, grey to brown with a dark line along the back and lighter underparts. The greater glider is over 3 ft long, of which the tail is over 1½ ft, grey to dark-brown with yellowish underparts. All live in trees and take gliding flights from tree to tree. The gliding membrane of the sugar glider is narrow, fringed with long hairs and stretches from the fore to the hind limbs. In the others this 'parachute' is a broader web of furred skin stretching from the 5th toe on the forefoot to the ankle of the hindleg. In the sugar glider the tail is feathered — that is, fringed either side with long hairs; in the remainder it is bushy.

Hidden in the tree tops

The feathertail flying phalanger, or glider, has the large eyes and ears typical of a nocturnal animal. It is seldom seen except when a tree is felled or a domestic cat brings one home. During the day it rests curled up in holes in trees, up to 50 ft from the ground, lying hidden in a nest of shredded eucalyptus bark. At night it takes gliding flights from tree to tree. It is said to be common wherever there are eucalyptus trees and especially those with a white smooth bark. In the trees it runs quickly over bark using its claws, and it can run over smooth leaves with the pads on the tips of the toes giving a sure grip.

The habits of sugar gliders and greater gliders are similar. When in the tops of the trees there is little to indicate they are moving about except a faint scratching on bark or the rustle of leaves. Their glides also are sudden and swift, usually seen only by accident. The gliding feats are most spectacular in the greater glider; one is recorded as having covered 590 yd in 6 successive glides, an average of nearly 100 yd between each pair of trees. During a glide the phalangers lose height, and having landed on the next tree they run rapidly up the trunk for the next takeoff. Sometimes one will land on the ground, over which it runs awkwardly.

All have a sweet tooth

The various flying phalangers differ in one respect: the teeth. The pigmy gliders have insectivorous teeth, recalling those of shrews. They eat insects and especially

Left: A sugar glider takes a snack. These pretty marsupials eat almost anything they can get.

△ *Takeoff; a well-judged launch into space . . .*
▽ *. . . and landing, gripping with sharp claws.*

plant lice, such as aphides and scale insects, that give out honeydew. The sugar glider also eats insects, and small birds as well, but its food is mainly flowers, fruit, buds, nectar and sap. The greater glider feeds only on leaves and flowers, mainly those of gum trees. Both these have the kind of teeth associated with a vegetarian diet.

Useful mobbing

Being marsupials, the females carry their young in a pouch, and when the babies are large enough to leave it they ride on the mother's back; at least this is true for the smaller species. This is known from only chance observation, as when a flying phalanger out in broad daylight was mobbed by a crowd of birds, including Australian magpies. One of these swooped and drove the phalanger hard against a tree. It hit its head on a branch and fell to the ground, where the baby fell from its back. Otherwise little is known of the breeding habits of these shy creatures. The pigmy glider has 2–4 young at a birth. The sugar glider has 1–3, usually 2, babies after a gestation of

953

3 weeks, the young becoming independent at 4 months. The greater glider has one young in July—August, which leaves the pouch at 4 months, but remains with the parents until fully grown.

Powerful owl enemy

The greatest hazard to flying phalangers lies in the steady felling of eucalyptus or gum trees. A phalanger occasionally falls victim to the introduced red fox when it lands on the ground. Otherwise the main enemies are owls, especially the one known as the powerful owl.

Bundles under the tail

Several marsupials use their tails for carrying nesting materials, and so does that other primitive mammal, the platypus. This is the more remarkable since the tail of a platypus is not long and slender but broad and flat—less suited, one would have thought, to being wrapped around a bundle of leaves. The rat kangaroos of Australia do the same, but their tails are prehensile, anyway. The American opossum brings its tail forward under the body, passes leaves and grass —or similar building materials—backwards under its chest, then with its hind legs arranges these for the tail to grasp. The greater glider has been recorded as carrying a bundle of twigs and leaves for a nest with its prehensile tail, and sugar gliders have been seen to do the same.

David Fleay, the Australian naturalist, watched a captive sugar glider hang by its hindfeet, bite leaves off eucalyptus boughs and, using the forepaws, transfer them to its tail. When it had a bundle about 6 in. long and 3 in. across, the phalanger ran along to its nesting box holding the burden with its tail wrapped round it.

Flattened, fur-clad skydivers

Below left: Sugar glider feeding on foliage. The folds of skin between the limbs give little idea of the massive 'parachute area' so dramatically illustrated below. The neatly-curled tail can be used for carrying nest material; Below: Study in unpowered flight. With only a leap from a treetrunk and the gliding effect of the outstretched skin, a flying phalanger can average 100 yd a trip, landing with remarkable accuracy some way up the trunk of a selected tree.

phylum	**Mammalia**
order	**Marsupialia**
family	**Phalangeridae**
genera & species	***Acrobates pygmaeus*** *pigmy glider* ***Petaurus australis*** *sugar glider* ***Schoinobates volans*** *greater glider*

▷ *Baby phalanger, blind, naked, and completely helpless, nestles in its mother's pouch. It will not become completely independent until about 4 months old.*

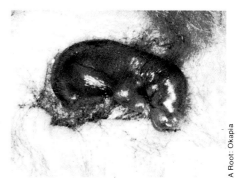

Flying squirrel

A squirrel making a seemingly miraculous leap from one tree to another is a common sight, but flying squirrels make proper flights, gliding from tree to tree.

There are 37 species, of which one is North American, one extends from southern Sweden through Finland and Siberia to Japan, and the rest live in southern and southeast Asia. All are similar in build and habits and all have a web of furred

dark slate or sepia fur, its tail feather-like and its flying membrane fringed with stiff hairs. The other Asiatic species are mainly around 2 ft total length, sometimes richly coloured, and varying from rufous to cream-coloured.

The only species whose biology is at all well known is the North American flying squirrel, and this is the one to which the name was originally given, by Captain John Smith who in 1624, in his Generall Historie of Virginia, *wrote: 'A small beaste they have . . . we call them flying*

Living magic carpets

Except during cold, wet and windy weather flying squirrels come out to feed at night, and travel from tree to tree by gliding with the four legs spread to stretch the flying membranes. On landing, a squirrel immediately races round to the other side of the tree, a precaution against attack from a predator while still recovering from the landing. Then the squirrel rapidly climbs to regain height lost in the glide. They rest by day in hollows in trees and will also use roof spaces, outbuildings and bird nesting-boxes. Occasionally the nest will

. . . with the greatest of ease: glide-in, braking and touchdown, all masterfully handled.

Series by Leonard Lee Rue III

skin on either side of the body extending from the foreleg to the hindleg and ending on the tail. The largest is the common giant flying squirrel of Asia (India, China, Taiwan to Indonesia), yellowish-grey to black above, white to yellow on the underside, measuring 4 ft overall. The next largest is the Kashmir giant flying squirrel, nearly 3 ft total length with soft, woolly greyish-fawn fur and a bushy tail. The smallest is the pigmy flying squirrel, of Malaya-Borneo, 5½ in. total length, with

squirrels.' Surprisingly, little is known of the habits of the so-called European flying squirrel (Sweden–Japan), but in size and appearance it is similar to the North American species, with its brownish coat and white to cream underparts, large eyes and small ears. The North American species will be dealt with here, and regarded as typical of the 35 other species. The North American flying squirrel is regarded by some zoologists as having two species, a southern and a northern.

be made on leafy branches, like the drey of tree squirrels, but more cosily lined. A nest is made of dry leaves, shredded bark, moss, feathers, and fur.

Their normal call is described as 'chuck-chuck-chuck' which changes to a squeal when the squirrel is alarmed or aggressive. At other times a musical chirping, sometimes slightly harsh, is used. It seems that some of their calls are in the ultrasonic range and it has been suggested that flying squirrels may use these (to a more limited extent) as bats do: to detect obstacles.

Impressive drinkers

The food of flying squirrels everywhere is much the same as that for the North American flying squirrel, which is nuts, seeds, fruits, lichen, fungi, bark and insects. Birds' eggs and small birds are sometimes taken. Food is hoarded by the North American species, which does not hibernate. It also is reputed to be a heavy drinker, so it locates itself near water. Will Barker, the American naturalist, claims that a flying squirrel will drink each night the equivalent of 2 gallons for a man.

Illar Muul has investigated the factors

This coincides with the ripening of the autumn harvest of nuts.

Nuts may be buried under leaves on the ground or pushed into cracks and crevices in trees. In the first the squirrel parts the leaf litter with its forepaws, pushes the nut between its hindlegs and, with tail erect, hammers it down with several blows of its snout. Nuts put into cracks in bark are hammered into place with the bare front teeth.

Illar Muul also investigated why, when the hoarding instinct is at its height, a squirrel makes no attempt to pick up nuts pre-

groups go into a state of semi-torpidity in which all activity declines.

Birth of a glider pilot

Breeding is from February to March or even later. After a gestation period of 40 days or more a litter of 2–6 is born. At birth the babies are naked, pink and blind, $2\frac{1}{2}$ in. long and weighing $\frac{1}{5}$ oz. The eyes open at 25–28 days. Weaning begins at 5 weeks.

Because they are almost wholly nocturnal the flying squirrels' main enemies are the larger owls.

that stimulate the hoarding of food. The favourite nuts of the North American flying squirrel are hickory nuts, with acorns second. In a good crop year 90% of its food will be hickory nuts. Some hoarding goes on at all times, fewer than 20 nuts a night in summer rising to a peak of 270 a night in November. The more intensive hoarding begins in mid-September, reaches a peak in November and drops back to fewer than 20 by mid-January. Tests suggest that it is the shortening of the period of daylight that triggers off the increased hoarding.

viously hoarded although it can see them. He suggests, as a result of his tests, that a secretion from glands on the infolded lips 'marks' each nut as the squirrel picks it up and carries it away to hoard it. Thereafter, such 'contaminated' nuts are ignored during the height of the hoarding season.

Another feature of the shortening day is that flying squirrels tend to rest in groups of up to two dozen in one nest. This is an advantage in that all keep warmer, but it also tends to make the hoarding a communal effort. During periods of bad weather these

Flight or gliding?

Those who write about animals are very ready to point out that the term 'flying squirrels' is a misnomer, that these animals do not truly fly like birds or bats, but only glide. This is apt to be misleading. The real difference is that in birds and bats we have *powered* flight, whereas in flying squirrels we have *controlled* flight without wing beats. To suppose they merely glide or parachute from tree to tree is far from the truth.

Before becoming airborne a flying squirrel

leans its head first to one side then to the other, possibly moving it up and down as well. In this it is using a form of triangulation to judge the distance and direction it must travel to its landing spot. When it does finally land it does so accurately, on the chosen spot. That this is not accidental is seen when a flying squirrel is disturbed and takes off hurriedly without assessing where it is going. It is then likely to land on the ground or even in water.

Just before landing the squirrel erects its tail, causing its head and body to rise vertically. This brings all 4 feet accurately on

rudder. A spur on each wrist joined to the flying membrane can be used to tighten or slacken the membrane. By dropping the legs of one side, to give added lift to the membrane on the other side, the squirrel can bank or turn sharply. It can also dive steeply and use the speed to rise steeply at the end of the dive.

Although most glides are simple, from one tree to another in a direct line, flying squirrels have been seen to make right-angled turns, lateral loops, spiral ascents and other aerobatics. They have even been seen to change their minds in mid-flight, turn com-

signalling whether to follow her, or stay while she makes an exploratory flight.

class	**Mammalia**
order	**Rodentia**
family	**Sciuridae**
genus & species	***Glaucomys volans*** *northern* **G. sabrinus** *southern North American flying squirrels others*

to the 'landing strip' to cushion the force of impact evenly, so the braked landing is gentle and the clawed toes are ready to grip the surface.

At the start of the flight, after deciding where it will make for, the squirrel leans forward, pushes with its hind legs and spreads all 4 legs at right angles to the body so the flying membranes on the 2 sides nearly form a square. It is then almost like a sheet of paper dropped horizontally from a tall building, but with more control.

The tail can be used as a balance and a

pletely around and land again on the exact spot from which they had just taken off.

The babies begin by making short flights at about a month old. Should one fall the mother will respond to its distress cries by flying down and retrieving it, picking it up by its membrane on one side with her mouth. At 6 weeks glides from branch to branch will be attempted, but for journeys from tree to tree the mother must coax her baby. Apparently she does much to train her offspring in the early stages, directing movements by signals, and especially

△ *Tense moment: an American flying squirrel prepares for its next glide. By cocking its head from side to side it judges distance and direction; then, extending its legs to spread the membrane and kicking off with the hindlegs, it leaps into space. The bushy tail and the spurs on the wrists are its controls: the tail forms a rudder and the spurs kink the membrane for turning and banking. An agile flier, its repertoire includes aerobatics like spiral ascents and flat loops. ▷ A flying squirrel at its night feeding, firmly suspended by the 'safety belt' fastenings of its sharp claws.*

Fossils

The age of the fossil dates from the end of the Pre-Cambrian era, about 570 million years ago. Scientific examination has revealed clear evidence of the existence of life at this time in the form of animal and plant fossils. About 4000 million years of the Cryptozoic age have already rolled by and we come now to the 340 million years of the Palaeozoic. There was a gap between the two periods, with the most ancient fossils of the Primary Era already showing species which, despite their great antiquity, are quite well evolved. The time lag between the blue algae or microscopic filamented organisms of the Pre-Cambrian era and the trilobites (a kind of fossil crustacean) of the early Cambrian period is, in fact, immense, and we will perhaps never know what the first animals and plants were. It is possible that they were too delicate to permit fossilization, or that the sediments of the period were too scanty to stand up to erosion and the geological changes which must have twisted them out of shape. The fact is that the portions of the Pre-Cambrian fossils which remain with us today are highly eroded, most frequently by successive periods of glaciation.

The Sedimentary beds

The geological history of the Earth is a long succession of the effects of internal forces thrusting outwards. These fall into the following categories: volcanic upheavals, orographic flexure (the formation of mountains), and epirogenic movements, which involve the raising and lowering of the level of the ground.

One of the consequences of these variations in the state of the Earth's surface has been the continual shifting of shorelines, through a constant series of marine transgressions and regressions (when the sea comes forward on to the land or retreats from it). Successive periods of freezing have added their influence to all these movements. The accumulation of immense surfaces of ice has loaded the polar caps, causing them to sink down, while at the same time reducing the volume of open water. When the ice began to melt, the effects were reversed. With the result that the oceans could vary as much as 300 to 600 ft in level.

Another cause of geological change (which applied purely to land) was the erosion caused by wind, frost and, above all, rain. Permanent wear and tear on everything, over the course of many thousands of years, piled up quantities of silt in the lower reaches of rivers and streams—with the finer particles descending the farthest and accumulating at the mouth of large rivers to form the bars of estuaries or deltas. All these processes ended in creating deposits of sediments in horizontal beds, or strata. If nothing happened to disrupt this slow sequence, over the course of millions of years, several beds would be superimposed one on top of another—with the oldest then becoming transformed by chemical, physical, or even biological forces. When this occurs in well defined stages, it is known as a stratigraphic series: A sedimentary cycle refers to a continuity of deposits between two marine regressions. The sedimentary beds which are richest in fossils are those deposited by marine transgressions, or by the drying up of swamps and marshes.

A large number of factors contribute to modify the basic plan of a typical stratigraphic series. One of the most important is the flexure caused by movements of the Earth's crust. The beds then cease to be horizontal. They are subjected to erosion at their surface and to new beds coming to cover them. These sort of modifications are called 'discordances'.

The object of stratigraphy is to reconstruct the history of the Earth in chronological

The history of life on Earth is based on the fossil evidence gleaned from the layers of sedimentary rocks. Modern dating techniques have allowed scientists to date rocks reasonably accurately and hence to construct a geological time scale.

EON	ERA	PERIOD	EPOCH	Millions of years ago	ANIMALS	PLANTS
PHANEROZOIC	CENOZOIC	QUATERNARY	HOLOCENE (RECENT)	0.01	Modern animals and man appeared.	Modern plants.
			PLEISTOCENE	1.8	Ice Ages in the northern hemisphere. Woolly mammals survived.	
		TERTIARY	PLIOCENE	6	Man's ape ancestors appeared. Many large mammals died out due to cold.	
			MIOCENE	22.5	Apes spread in Africa. Large herds of hooved mammals.	Grasslands spread.
			OLIGOCENE	38	First apes. Many hooved mammals and fierce carnivores.	Forest began to decrease at the end of the epoch.
			EOCENE	55	Early horses and elephants. Strange mammals, such as dinocerates and taeniodonts.	Ginkgos gradually declined. Forests covered much of the land.
			PALAEOCENE	65	Mammals began to spread after most of the reptiles had died out.	Flowering plants and conifers spread. Cycads declined.
	MESOZOIC	CRETACEOUS		135	Dinosaurs evolved into strange forms, but, together with the ammonites, died out at the end of the period.	First flowering plants appeared. Conifers and ginkgos spread. Bennettitaleans died out.
		JURASSIC		195	The age of dinosaurs and flying reptiles. First birds appeared, together with some small mammals.	Bennettitaleans and cycads flourished. Ferns, clubmosses and horsetails declined.
		TRIASSIC		230	Large sea reptiles. First dinosaurs and mammal-like reptiles. Ammonites abundant.	Bennettitaleans and cycads appeared.
	PALAEOZOIC	PERMIAN		280	Reptiles spread and amphibians declined. Trilobites became extinct.	Primitive conifers and ginkgos.
		CARBONIFEROUS		345	The age of amphibians. Reptiles evolved.	Luxuriant swamp forests that formed coal.
		DEVONIAN		410	The age of fishes. Ammonites and amphibians evolved.	Horsetails, clubmosses, ferns, seed ferns and cordaitales (gymnosperm ancestors).
		SILURIAN		440	Giant armoured fishes. Large sea scorpions.	First land plants (psilophytes) appeared. Mosses and liverworts possibly present.
		ORDOVICIAN		530	Jawless fish, the first vertebrates. Graptolites, trilobites, etc. abundant.	
		CAMBRIAN		570	Shells developed, so fossils abundant; e.g. graptolites, tribolites, molluscs, corals, crustaceans, echinoderms and brachiopods.	Algae.
PROTEROZOIC	PRE-CAMBRIAN			2600	Fossils rare, organisms probably all soft-bodied.	
CRYPTOZOIC				?	Life presumed to have been developing.	
ARCHAEOZOIC				?	Oldest known fossils — blue-green algae in rocks 3100 and 2800 million years old.	
AZOIC				4600	Life began 3000-4000 million years ago? Formation of the Earth.	

order. The great problem is, first of all, to determine the general changes through a number of local studies; then to make them fit into a comprehensive picture (which must take into account the varied conditions inherent in the different altitudes, continental locations at the time, and more or less equatorial or polar positions of the places considered – all while dealing with a host of other problems).

One of the practical results of this work is the establishment of so called palaeographic maps, which reconstruct the state of parts of the Earth at different periods.

Certain geological events have unfortunately managed to obliterate numerous sedimentary beds, or at the least rob them of fossils. These have mainly been tectonic movements (or changes relating to the surface of the Earth's crust), which have buried possible fossil beds at great depths. Internal pressure then subjected the beds to what is called metamorphism, which transformed them into crystalline rock. Alternatively, many of the oldest sediments, which have remained unburied since the Pre-Cambrian era, have over time been completely destroyed by erosion.

In general, the study of sedimentary beds has enabled us to establish a stratigraphic table – giving the logical succession of different stages, from the beginning of the Palaeozoic era, through the entire length of the fossil age. The stages are themselves grouped in 50 series, which are sub-divided into 'systems', corresponding to the different periods and times of each era – Primary, Secondary, Tertiary and Quaternary.

Through the comparative study of fossils, as well as various techniques of dating rocks, we have been able to draw up a chronological table to tie in with the stratigraphic one. As a result, we now have an increasingly precise outline of the Earth's past – in which every new discovery defines even more precisely our divisions of the 570 million years of prehistory.

Fossils – Nature's gift

The study of fossils is called palaeontology. Fossils exist at the heart of the most varied terrain. Sometimes they even form entire rocky beds all to themselves. As well as microlife, bacteria and protozoa, all sorts of animals and plants have been fossilized. The number of fossil species known today is enormous and constantly increasing – to the point that the experts reckon that it may soon exceed the number of species alive today.

In addition to animals and plants, many other things have been fossilized, including reptile eggs, coproliths (excrement), numerous animal tracks in light soil, and even burrows. Certain tracks of large dinosaurs have remained so well marked that they reveal the reptiles' posture and way of walking. We have even been able to determine the sites of battles between carnivorous and herbivorous dinosaurs.

The fossilization of ancient life forms has therefore left us invaluable evidence, the

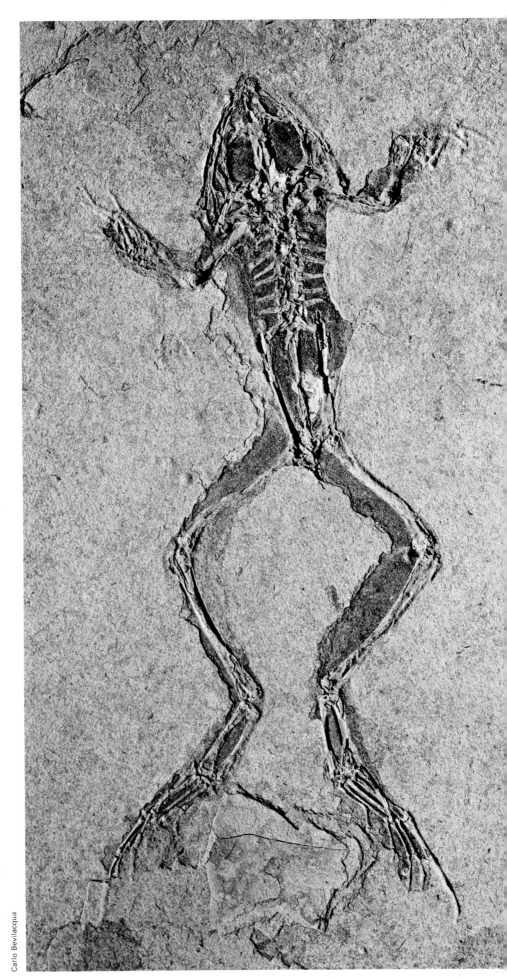

Rana pueyoi, *a superb fossil from the Miocene epoch, found in Spain. Frogs and toads appeared in the Jurassic period — 180 million years ago.*

Carlo Bevilacqua

study of which has not only helped us date the sedimentary beds, but shed light on the entire process of the evolution of life.

The process of fossilization

Both animals and plants decompose after death, if they remain exposed to the air. For a process of fossilization to begin, therefore, it must be protected from the action of the atmosphere. This can occur, either by straightforward burial in the earth, or by immersion in water. The action of different agencies then produces a transformation, which ensures the permanent conservation of the organism.

Fossilization by incrustation was a rapid process. It occurred in chalky streams whose deposits wrapped the animal round with a hard layer of limestone. Sediments composed of coarse rock are often rich in this kind of fossil.

Moulding occurred when the water's flow was extremely rapid. An external mould formed around a plant, which then broke up. If scientists inject a plastic into the cavities of the mould, then dissolve it, they can reconstruct the shape of the organism precisely. A great number of mollusc shells are known solely by their external mould. It often happened that once the body of the mollusc broke up, a fine sediment filled the resulting space and subsequently became solid – giving an inside to the shell.

Fossilization by mineralization was the most frequent process. Once an animal was buried in marine or lake sediments, its soft tissues would break up – and, simultaneously, its more durable parts would be invaded, molecule by molecule, by the mineral salts surrounding it. This kind of fossil is found in limestone, calcite, silica, chalcedony and phosphates. Ammonites (coil-shaped molluscs) have been fossilized by iron pyrites, more rarely by sulphur, and even by silver (in the mines of Peru).

Plants can go through this process also, and be so well preserved that, when the trunk of a fossilized tree has been sawn and polished, even its growth rings can be counted. All substances capable of resisting chemical agents after burial can be mineralized in their exact form – to the point where one can actually see the cellular layout of certain tissues.

Other types of fossilization, which are unfortunately more rare, preserve their organisms through a sort of mummification. Peat bogs are good examples of places termed 'antiseptically' suitable for this sort of transformation. Ancient wood extracts from the Australian peat bogs, for instance, have been sawn up and planed just as if they were recent trees. Other peat bogs have contained animals millions of years old, flattened and deformed, but preserved to the point where their cells can be examined under a microscope. Some animals have been abruptly covered by eruptions of lava. Nothing remains of them but the place where their bodies lay, and yet this shows the animal's shape in great detail (which can be extremely interesting – in the case of a rhinoceros, for example). It is equally possible to see just what a dinosaur's skin was like. For, when these creatures were covered by sand, it sometimes became a sort of press – which took on a faithful imprint of their hide.

Fossil insects

A great number of insects have been found coated in yellow amber in the Lebanon and around the Baltic Sea. Exactly where their resin came from is not known. But what is interesting about these fossils is the perfect way they have preserved the insects they contain. The fossil amber of the Lebanon is

Fossil of a marine gastropod of the genus Turritella. *In the process of fossilization, the mollusc's shell disintegrated, but inside it had become filled with fine sediment which preserved its shape.*

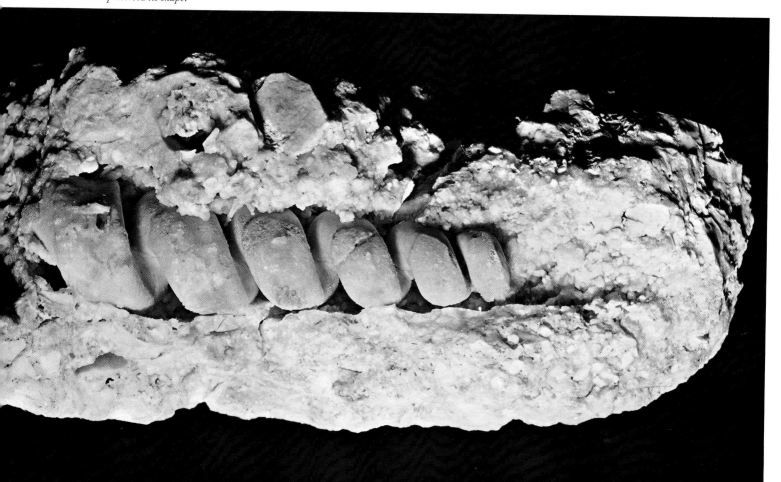

△Amber fossils from Lebanon and the Baltic Sea imprisoned and perfectly preserved many insects.

▽ Sedimentary rocks formed of very fine mud have kept the delicate impression of many fragile insects and spiders.

▽ Ammonites probably evolved in the Devonian period. They abounded in the seas for 300 million years until the end of the Cretaceous period. The evolution of these cephalopods can be traced throughout this time and thus they make excellent index fossils.

△Eoplatax papilio, *an Eocene batfish, discovered in northern Italy.*

◁△Cyathocrinus, *a crinoid or sea lily from the Silurian period.*

◁Astrangia, *a coral from North American Miocene rocks. This coral still exists.*

very old – 130 million years old – and thanks to it we know about the insects of the Mesozoic era.

Index fossils

Certain groups of animals are seen as a blessing by palaeontologists and geologists, who term them 'index fossils'. Among these are the ostracods, little crustaceans with a bivalve, or two-valved, shell. They are generally $3/1000$ in. to 1 in. long, though some species reach 2 in. A large number of sedimentary beds formed in water contain ostracods. The most ancient date from 500 million years ago. These crustaceans seem to have evolved rapidly, with different types and species following one another continuously through the ages. Each geological epoch possesses its typical ostracods, which are perfectly distinct from those which come before or after it – and studying them allows one to date the land where they are found. As a result of the differences in their shells, one can also deduce what their environment was like: its water well or badly oxygenated, fresh, or more or less salty.

Other index fossils, such as the ammonites, stand out as landmarks in the history of life. These 'cephalate' (sucker-headed) molluscs must have abounded in the Mesozoic era, as nearly 10 000 species of them are known. The shape of their shell is

△ *Three views of a fossil trilobite that died in the rolled-up position.*

▷ *Overleaf:* Seymouria baylorensis, *from North American Permian rocks, was an amphibian that also had some characteristics of both fish and reptiles.*

characterized by the way it curls, rather like a ram's horn. Many were only about an inch in diameter, but the largest reached 8 ft. The ammonites disappeared at the end of the Cretaceous period, 65 million years ago, and their only present day relative is the rare nautilus. The most primitive form of ammonite dates from the Devonian period of the Palaeozoic era. Throughout their long existence, these molluscs have evolved morphologically (by biological changes), with each period having its typical families. They were essentially sea creatures, frequenting warm waters. So the presence of beds of ammonite fossils high in mountains, or deep in the interior of continents, tells us a great deal about marine transgressions and regressions.

The trilobites are also index fossils. Of great antiquity, these first arthropods made good fossils due to their chitinous shells. They already existed at the very beginning of the Cambrian period – counting among the first known animals – and were extinct at the end of the Palaeozoic era. The trilobites lived on the ocean floor and were spread throughout the seas of the world. We are acquainted with more than 1000 species of them. Many were extremely small, though the largest grew to a length of over 2 ft. Right through the 300 million years of their existence, these animals evolved morphologically – and so provide an invaluable yardstick with which to date ancient times.

There is insufficient space here to show the immense value of other specific groups of fossils in helping one deduce what conditions were like in their place and times. But, in general, fossils enable us not only to understand both plant and animal evolution, but also to deduce the vertical movements of the Earth's crust as well as variations in climate and temperature – even the composition of the atmosphere itself. And even when they only confirm other methods of dating they are of value, as they thereby prove how reliable those methods are.

▽ *In the Carboniferous and Permian periods fossils were formed in coal, giving us many detailed impressions of the vegetation of that time.*

▽ *The skeleton of an ichthyosaur. This huge marine reptile left a number of impressive fossils in the sedimentary beds of the Mezozoic era.*

Four-eyed fish

This remarkable fish has two eyes each divided into two. Even more remarkable, 'left-handed' males must mate with 'right-handed' females and vice versa.

A minnow-like fish, 6—8 in. long, sometimes reaching 1 ft, it lives in fresh-water from southern Mexico through central America to northern South America. It is long-bodied with a rounded tail fin but otherwise undis-tinguished in shape except for its large goggling eyes. It spends most of its time cruising at the surface with only the upper half of each eye above the water.

Divided eyeballs

Each eye of the four-eyed fish is divided horizontally by a partition, and the fish swims with the surface of the water level with this. The partition divides the cornea. Anything underwater is seen by the upper retina through the lower cornea. Vision through water requires a thicker lens than vision through air, so the lens is oval, and anything viewed underwater is seen through the thicker part of it.

Land animals have a tear duct to keep the eye moist but the four-eyed fish has to dip its head from time to time to keep its eyes from drying out.

Looking for prey

The four-eyed fish feeds on small swimming animals. It would be reasonable to suppose that with the double vision it could look for food under the surface and also for any insects falling on the water. This, however, seems to be in some doubt. Its usual way of feeding is to swim down, catch its prey, then immediately swim up to lie once again just under the surface with half of each eye above the waterline. We can only suppose also that its aerial vision helps in keeping watch for enemies from above, such as water-birds.

Compatible marriage

The females bear between 1—5 living young. One female 6 in. long gave birth to one baby $2\frac{1}{2}$ in. long, and another of similar size gave birth to 4, each of which was $1\frac{1}{2}$ in. long. Fertilisation is internal; the male must inject his sperms into the female. He does this using a tube formed from modified rays of the anal fin. In any male this tube can only be moved either to the left or to the right.

The sexual opening of the female is pro-tected by a special scale, so it can be entered only from the left or from the right. As a result a 'left-handed' male can mate only with a 'right-handed' female, and vice versa.

Bifocal blenny

Anableps anableps and *A. tetrophthalmus*, the two species of four-eyed fishes so far dis-cussed, are not alone. There is a four-eyed blenny, 3 in. long, living on the rocky shores of the Galapagos Islands. Its eyes are di-vided by a vertical partition, and for a long

Two-tier vision: the compound eyes of the four-eyed fish scan both air and water.

time we have been told that this blenny spends much of its time in a vertical position with its nose out of water and the partition in the eye coinciding with the waterline. In 1963, however, the German zoologist, Ebe-hard Curio, studied this blenny *Dialommus fuscus* at first-hand in the Galapagos and found it does no such thing. It feeds on small crustaceans and it comes out onto rocks at low tide. It has a skilful way of moving about. The blenny rides the crest of a wave and lets this wash it into a crevice. If the crevice is unsuitable the blenny moves over the wet rock with sculling movements of its tail. When returning to the sea it waits for the run-off to carry it back. This and more Curio learned, but he could not find out what use were the 'four eyes'.

Although *Anableps* was the first fish to be called four-eyed the only one that truly deserves the name was brought up from deep water in the North Pacific only a few years ago. Given the name *Bathylychnops exilis*, it is a slender pike-like fish, $1\frac{1}{2}$ ft long, living in the twilight zone of blue light, between 300 and 3 000 ft down. From its shape it is a hunter that catches other fishes by short swift spurts. It needs good eyesight and the large eye has a retina made up of millions of rods, the light-sensitive cells. This gives wide vision and also keen sight for detail. Each large eye has a small eye on its lower part which looks downwards. These have their own retina and probably give greater sensitivity, especially in judging distances. Behind the small eyes are two smaller eye-like organs that are no more than swellings on the cornea of the large eye. They lack a retina and probably do no more than bend the light rays into the large eye. Yet this is only a guess and we may have to wait a long time for an explanation why such an unusual fish exists with four eyes on each side of its head.

class	**Osteichthyes**
order	**Atheriniformes**
family	**Anablepidae**
genus & species	*Anableps anableps others*

Root/Okapia

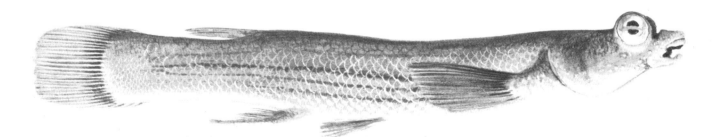

Malcolm McGregor

Anableps anableps, *the freshwater four-eyed fish of central America (actual size).*

Francolin

Francolins are birds very like partridges or quails, to which they are related. They are among the largest of the pheasant family, reaching 18 in. long and weighing up to 3½ lb. Compared with some of their relatives, most francolins have dull colours, but their plumage is beautifully patterned. In a few the male is brightly coloured, but as is usual in this family, the female is always sombrely coloured. Like quail, francolins have a squat, rounded body, small head and short tail. They have sharp spurs, like those of domestic cockerels, and some male francolins have two on each leg.

There are 40 species, 36 living in Africa and 5 in Asia. A few are widespread, such as the bush fowl of West Africa and the black francolin, which ranges from Assam to Cyprus and once lived as far west as Spain. Francolins live in wooded or brush country, not in arid plains or thick forests. In Asia they are found both on the plains and in the hills, including the lower slopes of the Himalayas, as high as 7 000 ft.

Difficult to find

Francolins are shy, secretive birds, keeping to long grass or undergrowth and rarely flying. When they do take off they fly low with whirring wings, like other members of the family. They generally live in small coveys of 5 or 6 birds, retiring at night to roost in trees. In years gone by francolins were highly regarded as gamebirds, so most accounts of them have been written from the point of view of the sportsman. They have been variously described as 'probably the best gamebird in Somaliland' or as offering 'pretty sport . . . 50 brace may be bagged in a single day by a single sportsman'. Such a sportsman must have been very painstaking because other reports show how difficult it was to find the birds and to flush them. They can be seen darting across open ground, but once they have found cover they are difficult to locate, crouching motionless, blending in perfectly with their background. They have even been credited with being able to elude the best dogs by arranging their feathers to prevent their scent from spreading. This story is hard to believe but it certainly shows their impressive ability to hide.

One way of locating francolins is to listen for their noisy calls, which range from harsh croaks to tinkling chirrups. Cock francolins begin to call at dawn; as one starts up others nearby immediately join in. Calling continues intermittently all day and is heard especially after showers of rain. The calls, however, appear to have a ventriloquial quality and both hunters and bird watchers have reported wandering around in circles in fruitless endeavours to find a calling francolin.

Scratching a living

Francolins scratch for food on the ground like domestic chickens, scraping back leaf litter and soil with their stout claws and pecking up the small animals, plants and so on that are uncovered. They will dig for bulbs buried 2 in. deep. Their favourite feeding grounds appear to be in clearings, where they can easily scratch at the surface. They feed mainly in the early morning and evening, but during the rainy season they feed all day, when food is especially abundant. Ants and termites are especially favoured, and francolins also eat snails, beetles and spiders, together with seeds, fruit and the tender green tips of plants.

Pairs keep to themselves

At the beginning of the breeding season the small coveys of francolins split into pairs, each of which sets up its own territory. Ownership of a territory is advertised by calling, sometimes with male and female calling in a duet. In South Africa Hartlaub's francolin nests on kopjes. These are piles of boulders about 50 ft high that are scattered about the flat plains. There is one pair of francolins to each kopje, which start to call from the topmost rock just before sunrise. As the sun climbs higher in the sky, the calls gradually die away.

The nest is little more than a scrape in the ground, sometimes lined with leaves. The usual clutch is 5–6 eggs in some species and up to a dozen in others. They are incubated by the female alone for about 20 days. The chicks leave the nest·very soon and are looked after by both parents.

Danger from fire

It is very unlikely that only man finds francolins worth hunting. All they have to protect them is their shyness and ability to hide in thick cover, and their reluctance to take flight again once flushed. Bush or forest fires are a particular menace to their safety. These are most common during the breeding season, taking a toll of the eggs and chicks, and by destroying the cover they rob.francolins of their main protection.

Slender evidence

The first specimen of the Somali greywing francolin was collected by the British explorer JH Speke in 1855, just a few years before he discovered the source of the River Nile at Lake Victoria. At the time, however, this specimen was thought to belong to another species. It was not given its proper place in the classification of francolins until some years later. Then Lort Phillips, an American collector, found a freshly-killed francolin. Its head was missing but the wings were intact with their feathers still in place. The colouring seemed unusual so he took it home with him and it failed to match up with any specimen in the museum collections. Accordingly Lort Phillips fitted out another expedition to the Wagar Mountains in what was then Somaliland to look for this francolin, which was eventually named after him.

This account is perhaps rather trivial and of no great interest but it does show how much times have changed. Lort Phillips lived in the heyday of the animal collector. It seems incredible now that men had the money and the leisure to make a special trip to Africa, no easy business in those days, to search for an animal whose existence was based on the remains of a predator's feast. It is not even as if the animals were of any particular scientific or popular interest.

class	**Aves**
order	**Galliformes**
family	**Phasianidae**
genus & species	***Francolinus francolinus*** *black francolin* **F. hartlaubii** *Hartlaub's francolin* **F. lorti** *Somali greywing francolin* **Pternistis leucoscepus** *yellow throated francolin* *others*

Like their relatives the partridges and quails, francolins make first-class gamebirds; they live in open country and grow up to 3½ lb, ranking among the largest of the pheasant family. Most of them have a dull, brownish basic colour but some—like the yellow-throated francolins (opposite)—sport bright patches of colour on head and neck.

Arthur Christiansen

Frigatebird

Frigatebirds or Man-o'-war birds are the pirates of the seas. They are related to boobies, cormorants and darters, and although they feed on seafood and live by coasts, they can hardly be called seabirds. Frigatebirds have become almost as well adapted to an aerial way of life as the swifts. Their legs are so weak they can only walk with difficulty and need to leap from a tree or rock to become airborne. Their feet bear only the vestiges of webs and their plumage is not very waterproof, so they are helpless on the water. They have, however, an enormous wingspan, over 7 ft in the larger species, on which to support a mere 3 or 4 lb body. They have a larger wingspan/weight ratio than albatrosses and consequently are masters of gliding and soaring in the slightest breezes.

The silhouette of an airborne frigatebird is unmistakable, with long, pointed wings, a 4in. hooked bill and a deeply-forked tail. The plumage is mainly black, shot with blue or green. Males have a red throat pouch.

Frigatebirds are found in the warm oceans, especially where flying fish are abundant but they sometimes stray farther north or south; in 1953 one was seen in the Hebrides.

Coastal homes

Unlike albatrosses and many other sea-birds, frigatebirds do not leave their nesting colonies outside the breeding season to make long voyages over the oceans. They are occasionally seen 500 or more miles from land, but it can usually be assumed that if several frigatebirds are seen together, land cannot be far away. Their attachment to the breeding colony has been exploited in the islands of the Pacific Ocean, where frigatebirds are tamed and used like homing pigeons for carrying messages.

The Ancient Greeks considered the frigatebird to be the most aerial of birds. The swifts probably take pride of place, but the ability of frigatebirds to hover effortlessly or to soar for hours on end in air currents swirling up over cliffs is most impressive. Coupled with this, they can fly with the speed of a falcon and manoeuvre with incredible agility, using their forked tails as rudders.

Aerial highwaymen

For part of their time frigatebirds are pirates and robbers, stealing from other seabirds as they carry food back to their chicks. Boobies and gannets, and to a lesser extent noddies and tropic birds are harried by the swift-flying frigatebirds until, in desperation, they drop their food and escape. Immediately the frigatebirds swoop to catch the food before it hits the sea and sinks. The frigate-birds circle round the victim, pecking at its wings and tail and sometimes capsizing it. They are very persistent and the tormented bird can escape only by dropping its load or seeking refuge amongst trees. On

JB Nelson: Photo Res.

John Warham

JB Nelson: Photo Res.

Scenes in the life of the Man-o'-war bird

◁ *Top: Only child — a great frigatebird chick. It is cared for by both parents and depends on them for some 11 months before it learns all the aerobatic tricks of the frigatebird's trade and can fend for itself.*

Centre: Mature relation — an adult lesser frigatebird. Notice the enormous length of the wings compared with the size of the body.

Bottom: Gawky adolescent — a youthful frigatebird sunning itself on the rocks, inclining its outspread wings to let the sun catch their undersurfaces.

▷ *A frigatebird squadron sweeps in to drink at 'Frigate Pool' on South Island, Aldabra, in the Indian Ocean. Tortoises have preceded them.*

▽ *Father's return — a male frigatebird touches down at his nest on Tower Island, Galapagos.*

CA Wright

Philippa Scott: Photo Res.

occasions, however, frigatebirds will break off their attack. It seems they can recognise from the cries the bird makes whether it is worth harassing or not, for stifled cries of alarm mean a cropful of fish.

Throughout the tropics it is rare to find a colony of seabirds that does not have its attendant frigatebirds patrolling offshore for parent birds returning to the nests. Piracy is a major source of food only during the breeding season, as the colonies are empty for the rest of the year and the birds spread over the ocean. For most of the year, frigatebirds must catch their own

means that pairs breed at different times, so a frigatebird may find its nest has been occupied by another pair while it was away recovering from the previous breeding season.

An unusual feature of courtship is that the males are not aggressive at the start of breeding. As a result they can sit together and display communally, so providing a strong stimulus to passing females. When courting, a male half opens his wings and inflates his throat pouch, which looks like a red balloon under his chin. During this period its colour becomes a brighter red.

swoop and carry them off if their parents neglect them for a moment.

Precision aerobatics

To snatch flying fish from the sea or food from a booby needs split-second timing and an incredible judgement of distances that must be the envy of pilots in display teams. The Cossack trick of picking a handkerchief from the ground with the teeth while riding a horse is child's play compared with the frigatebirds' skill. Bryan Nelson, who studied frigatebirds on the Galapagos,

Like a stack of gliders at a sailplane rally: frigatebirds wheel in a thermal (a rising air current) over Tower Island in the sun-baked Galapagos Islands.

Philippa Scott: Photo Res

food, they swoop and snatch fish, squid, jellyfish or other planktonic animals that live on or just below the surface. They also take a heavy toll of newly hatched turtles as they struggle down the beaches and swim out to sea. Whole broods of turtles, numbering 100 or more, may perish before reaching the water's edge, as the frigatebirds swoop down and pick them up in their bills. The only hope of survival is for these turtles to hatch at night and disperse well out to sea before daybreak brings the frigatebirds back.

A long adolescence
Frigatebirds breed on the coasts of oceanic islands, often among colonies of boobies or other birds, from whom they steal not only food but also eggs and chicks. The nests of sticks, feathers and bones are built in trees or bushes. So adept are frigatebirds at flying that they tear dead twigs off trees while airborne.

The breeding period lasts much longer than that of any of their relatives, and like the wandering albatross, frigatebirds nest only every other year. They are not so faithful to their nest sites as other seabirds; because they breed every other year it

When a female comes near, the males shiver and rattle their feathers.

A single white egg is laid and incubated by both parents in shifts of 10−15 days. The egg hatches in 55 days and the chick is cared for by both parents. In the great frigatebird of the Galapagos, if not others, there follows a very long period of dependence on the parents. They spend 5 months on the nest and then another 6 months in being fed by the parents while themselves learning to feed. This appears to be necessary because the food supply is erratic and because it takes a long time for the young to learn the extreme skills needed to catch their food. They gather in small flocks, swooping on sticks or feathers and so gradually learn how to snatch flying fish or baby turtles. So difficult is this technique that many young frigatebirds die of starvation after their parents have stopped feeding them.

Their own worst enemies
As they live on small islands, frigatebirds have few enemies. The Galapagos short-eared owl, however, preys on the chicks there, but generally the chicks' worst enemies are other frigatebirds, who will

records how he saw a frigatebird swoop at full speed towards a rock. As it hurtled past it bent its neck and wiped a thin smear of fish from the rock, making a faint click with its bill. On another occasion a frigatebird took a piece of fish from the sand. Examination showed that the surface of the sand had not been disturbed in the slightest. Similar control is needed for another trick of the frigatebirds. One will sometimes wait for the moment when a booby is about to feed its chick, then swoop down, knocking the boobies apart and taking the food from whichever booby has it in its bill. Moreover a frigatebird will play the same trick on others of its kind.

class	**Aves**
order	**Pelecaniformes**
family	**Fregatidae**
genus & species	***Fregata aquila*** *Ascension Island frigatebird* ***F. magnificens*** *magnificent frigatebird* ***F. minor*** *great frigatebird*

Frilled lizard

One of the so-called dragons of Australia, the frilled lizard grows to about 3 ft long, with a slender body and long tail. It is pale brown, either uniformly coloured or with patches of yellow and darker brown. Its most conspicuous feature is the frill around the throat, like the ruff fashionable in Europe in the Middle Ages.

Apart from its size the only remarkable thing about this lizard is its frill. Normally this lies folded over the shoulders like a cape. It is a large area of skin supported by cartilaginous rods from the tongue bone which act like the ribs of an umbrella. In moments of excitement, muscles pulling on these raise the frill to 8 in. or more across, about as wide as the length of the head and body together.

It lives mainly in sandy semi-dry areas of northern and northeastern Australia.

Hindleg sprinter

The frilled lizard lives in rough-barked trees, coming to the ground after rainstorms, to feed. When disturbed on the ground it runs on its hindlegs with the frill laid back over the shoulders, tail raised, and the forelegs held close into the body. It may sprint for a considerable distance, or it may seek safety by climbing a tree. When brought to bay it turns, opens its mouth wide and extends its frill. The best description of what happens next is given by Harry Frauca in *The Book of Australian Wild Life*. It does not raise its tail, as it has often been reported to do, and as some other similar lizards are known to do, but keeps it flat on the ground. It sways from side to side and with its open mouth, coloured dark blue inside edged by pinkish yellow, surrounded by the greenish-yellow frill splashed with red, brown, white and black, it looks like a large flower among broad leaves. The colours of the lizard vary from one region to another. In Queensland the general colour is a sombre grey, in the Northern Territory it is pinkish, often with a black chest and throat. The colours of the mouth and frill also vary.

The open mouth and spread frill are a warning display. If the warning is ignored it passes to an aggressive display. The lizard steps boldly towards the intruder, keeping its mouth open and frill fully extended, and from the mouth comes a low hiss. The remarkable thing is that people who know very well the lizard can do nothing to harm them, tend nevertheless to be intimidated by all this show. Even a dog used to attacking larger lizards will retreat before it.

Meals of ants and eggs

The frilled lizard eats insects, including large quantities of ants, as well as spiders and small mammals. It is also said to be an egg thief. One of the many difficulties found in keeping this animal in captivity is that of getting enough of the right kind of food. In 1893, when the time it took to travel from Australia to Great Britain was much longer than it is today, the naturalist

Root/Okapia

△ *Defiance: a cornered lizard unfurls its frill.*

W Saville Kent brought a frilled lizard to London, the first to reach Europe alive. When it was exhibited before an audience of learned gentlemen one eminent zoologist is said to have followed it, in his excitement, on hands and knees, to watch it careering round on its hind legs and displaying its frill. Unfortunately, there is no record of how Saville Kent managed to feed his pet, but, like many reptiles, the frilled lizard can probably go without food for months.

Universal umbrella trick

Neither does history record whether any of the learned gentlemen noticed a comparison between the lizard and a lady. At that time ladies carried parasols and it was not uncommon for a lady, confronted by a cow as she crossed a field, to frighten the cow away by suddenly opening her parasol in its face. Konrad Lorenz, in *King Solomon's Ring*, tells how his wife kept geese from devastating her newly-planted flower beds. She carried a large scarlet umbrella and this she would suddenly unfold at the geese, with a jerk, causing the geese to take to the air with a thundering of wings. It is almost instinctive for a woman carrying an umbrella to use it in this way against a power-

ful and persistent opponent. It is a matter of no small interest to find that this same effective defence should have been evolved by a lizard.

class	**Reptilia**
order	**Squamata**
suborder	**Sauria**
family	**Agamidae**
genus & species	*Chlamydosaurus kingii*

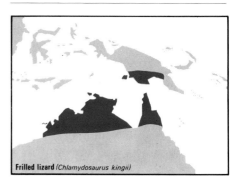

Frilled lizard *(Chlamydosaurus kingii)*

973

Frilled shark

This rare and little known shark, of which there is only one species, takes us back in imagination nearly 500 million years. The earliest known fossils of vertebrates were of fish-like animals without jaws and with sucking mouths. The first relics of modern fishes, though still very primitive, are first found in 400-million-year-old rocks. At a later date they began to separate out into sharks and true or bony fishes — and the frilled shark is very like the fossils of these earliest sharks.

The frilled shark is 6½ ft long, a uniform brown and eel-like, with a single dorsal fin set far back on its body. The outstanding feature that gives it its name is the six gills with their frilly margins on each side of the head—a feature shared with the earlier sharks. With few exceptions.all modern sharks have five pairs of gills.

While most species of shark have been known for a long time, the frilled shark came to light less than a century ago. The first specimens were brought up from deep water by Japanese long-line fishermen, some of whom called it **ribuka** *(silk shark) and others,* **tokagizame** *(lizard shark). The first name was probably based on the thin, almost silk-like fins, the second on its general appearance.*

Another living fossil

The frilled shark has various primitive characters in addition to its six frilled gills. Its mouth is terminal, that is, at the front of the head. In modern sharks the mouth is on the underside, so the snout and upper jaw overhang it. The jutting snout forms a cutwater which makes for increased speed, so we have to assume the frilled shark is not a speedy swimmer. The nostrils of the frilled shark are on the upper side of the head whereas in modern sharks they are on the underside. In modern sharks the tail has two lobes to the tail fin, a long upper and a smaller lower lobe. In the frilled shark there is no lower lobe and the tail as a whole trails horizontally instead of

curving upwards. All these things suggest a lethargic swimmer, and so do the frilled gills. In these the gills themselves, instead of being deep in the gill-cavity, are almost outside, virtually on the edge of the frill. There is also a curtain of skin behind the back teeth. This probably acts as a valve so, whereas other sharks must keep swimming to breathe, the frilled shark—like bony fishes—can breathe by pumping water through the gills while stationary.

The teeth of the early sharks had many small pointed cusps, giving a comb-like effect. The living frilled shark's teeth have three pointed cusps with two smaller ones between, which is more than most modern sharks have. Other differences are that all the teeth are in use at once whereas in other sharks only those in front are functional. When these are broken, they are replaced by new teeth growing up and forward, on the conveyor-belt principle. The teeth of the frilled shark are in rows of fives, each row on its own plate. and there are 20-27 such rows in both upper and lower jaws.

The lateral line running down the flanks of true or bony fishes consists of a series of sense-organs, each opening by a pore, so that each sense-organ is embedded in the skin. In most living sharks the sense-organs are in a tube embedded in the skin. In the frilled shark the lateral line is an open groove with the sense-organs lying in it, as in the earliest known sharks.

Recent arrival

Frilled sharks live in deep water, in the Atlantic and on both sides of the Pacific, down to 1 800 ft. They are harmless to man in spite of the wicked gaping mouth. For one thing they live below the depths to which divers go, and they feed solely on deepwater octopuses and squids, according to the distinguished South African ichthyologist JLB Smith, 'discoverer' of the coelacanth. He pointed out that the teeth all point backwards, like those of a snake. The gape of the mouth is wide, and the jaws are distensible, as in a snake, so Smith is not surprised the Japanese saw some resemblance to a reptile, even if they called it lizard rather than snake.

Smith presumes that once a frilled shark seizes its prey it has no chance of escape. The shark holds it, slowly working it back-

wards—pulling itself over its prey, so to speak. Such a feeding method is best suited to eating octopus and squid, rather than fishes coated with scales. Certainly the Japanese fishermen used squid for bait.

Because no frilled shark yet caught has had food in its stomach, or at best only a small quantity of semi-digested remains, Professor Smith suggests that, having eaten a large squid or octopus, the frilled shark lies on the bottom like a gorged python and ignores the bait.

One final clue to its feeding habits may be in its eyes. These can, according to Professor Smith, be protruded a little from their sockets and rotated upwards; only a bottom-living animal having to keep watch above for food or foes would need such an adaptation.

Prolonged motherhood

The female frilled shark lays eggs that hatch just before they reach the exterior. Each egg is oval, nearly 5 in. long, and one female may deliver up to 15 babies after a gestation of nearly 2 years.

Links in the chain

There are quite a number of deep-sea sharks but only one with six frilled gills. One other modern shark has six gills and a few have seven. Some of these sharks live in shallow seas, others in deep seas. The one species with six gills is *Hexanchus griseus*. It may be 17 ft long, and one of 26 ft in length was caught off Cornwall more than a century ago. Together with the several species of seven gill sharks, they are placed in a family on their own, the Hexanchidae. All have comb teeth but their mouths are on the underside of the head. They are primitive but are newcomers compared with the frilled shark, because the first fossils almost identical with them are found in rocks laid down a mere 100 million years ago.

class	**Chondrichthyes**
order	**Hexanthiformes**
family	**Chlamydoselachidae**
genus & species	***Chlamydoselachus anguineus***

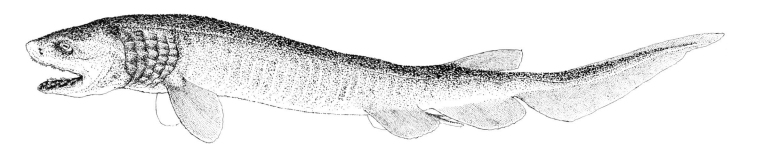

Dun-coloured, eel-like, the rare frilled shark is 6½ ft long with its dorsal fin set far back on its body. It got its name from the six gills with their frilly margins.

Fritillary

Fritillary butterflies owe their name to a genus of plants **Fritillaria** *whose flowers have a dark and light chequered pattern. Certain butterflies of the family Nymphalidae have a similar pattern on their wings and were named 'fritillaries' by the early entomologists. Nearly all have the upperside of the wings reddish-yellow with black spots or chequers and the underside more variously patterned. The British usage of the name includes members of two subdivisions or 'tribes', the Argynnidi and the Melitaeidi; in America only the former are called fritillaries, the latter being known as 'checkerspots', and the distinction is a useful and logical one. Most of the argynnid or 'true' fritillaries have a pattern of metallic silvery markings on the underside of the hind wings, most beautifully developed in the Queen of*

△ *Glanville fritillary larva* **Melitea cinxia**.

Spain fritillary. Metallic markings are never found in the melitaeids or checkerspots.

The larvae of both groups have rows of finely branched spines on their bodies and they pupate by hanging themselves up by the tail, as in all the butterflies of the large family Nymphalidae to which the fritillaries belong.

Localised colonies

Fritillaries are mainly woodland butterflies, the silver-washed, high brown and the two pearl-bordered fritillaries being especially characteristic of mixed woodland in which oak and birch predominate. The dark green fritillary flies on downs, moors, and open grassy country. The Queen of Spain fritillary is a very rare vagrant to the south of England; in continental Europe it is found both in woods and flowery meadows. Of the three British 'checkerspots', the marsh fritillary haunts marshes and damp meadows

and the Glanville lives on chalk downs. All three tend to form small localised colonies, many of which have been exterminated in recent years; in Britain the Glanville fritillary is confined to the Isle of Wight.

Fritillaries frequent flowers but are seldom seen in gardens unless these border on or are surrounded by woods. They are highly characteristic of the temperate and cool zones of the Northern Hemisphere. Both groups are well represented in North America and in Europe, whence they extend

△▽ *Gulf fritillary* **Dione juno** *emerges . . .*

across Asia to Japan. A few species are among the most northern of all butterflies. The Arctic fritillary *Clossiana chariclea* is circumpolar in distribution and has been found at 81 degrees 42 minutes north latitude.

The few that occur south of the equator are nearly all mountain butterflies and are regarded as relict species which probably crossed the tropics in the cool conditions of the Ice Age. Three of these occur at altitudes of over 6 000 feet in Africa; they are members of the genus *Issoria,* related to the

Queen of Spain fritillary. Another genus *Yramea* is represented by a number of species along the Andean mountain range in South America; they are intermediate in their characters between the true fritillaries and the checkerspots. There is only one truly tropical fritillary *Argyreus hyperbius* which is widespread in the Oriental Region and extends to New Guinea and eastern Australia.

No butterflies in winter

All the British fritillaries have one generation in the year, and all but one pass the winter as larvae; the exception is the high brown, which winters as an egg. The caterpillars of the silver-washed and dark green fritillaries hatch from the egg in August and immediately go into hibernation without feeding. They begin to feed in the spring, on wild violet, and pupate in June or July, and the butterflies emerge after 2 or 3 weeks. These two and the high brown (the three 'large' British fritillaries) fly from July to early August. The larvae of the two pearl-bordered fritillaries hibernate

△ *. . . and spreads its wings to harden and dry.*

when nearly fully grown, pupate in the spring and the butterflies are on the wing in May and June, the small pearl-bordered rather later than the other. All three of the checkerspots (marsh, heath and Glanville) have a long larval life of 10–11 months, passing through their other stages quickly in the early or middle part of the summer. The larvae of the marsh fritillary hibernate communally in a web.

Different feeding habits

The larger species that fly after midsummer suck nectar from various flowers, thistles and bramble being among their favourites. The two pearl-bordered fritillaries are late spring butterflies; the blue woodland flower called bugle often coincides with them both in locality and season, and seems to be their chief source of food.

In their choice of larval food plants the two groups differ. The true fritillaries almost all feed on violets or closely related plants such as violas and pansies. The

checkerspots on the other hand range widely in their food plants, but each species is usually confined to a particular plant species or genus, a habit that must be at any rate partly responsible for their occurring in localised colonies. Of the British species the Glanville fritillary feeds on certain species of plantain, the heath on cow-wheat and the marsh on devil's-bit scabious.

A question of madness

John Ray (1627-1705) was Britain's first true naturalist. In his *Historia Insectorum* he gives the species we know as the pearl-bordered fritillary the name April fritillary. This seems quite inappropriate as the butterfly hardly ever appears before the beginning of May. A change of climate might have occurred, but the probable explanation is that Ray lived before the change in the calendar that took place in 1752. In that year 11 days were omitted in order to bring British practice into line with the Gregorian Calendar of continental Europe. This resulted in an 11-day shift of dates relative to the seasons; before it took place the pearl-bordered fritillary must regularly have appeared in Britain before the end of April.

The name of the Glanville fritillary commemorates a curious story. In the early part of the 18th century a well-to-do lady of this name was among the early butterfly collectors. Women who did such things then were regarded as somewhat eccentric, and when Lady Glanville died her will was disputed by some disappointed relatives on the ground that because she collected butterflies she must have been mad! The case went to court, but it is pleasant to record that her reputation for sanity was upheld and that the greedy relations incurred trouble and expense to no purpose.

class	**Insecta**
order	**Lepidoptera**
family	**Nymphalidae**

British fritillaries
Tribe Argynnidi

Argynnis paphia	*silver-washed fritillary*
A. cydippe	*high brown fritillary*
A. aglaia	*dark green fritillary*
Issoria lathonia	*Queen of Spain fritillary*
Clossiana euphrosyne	*pearl-bordered fritillary*
C. selene	*small pearl-bordered fritillary*

Tribe Melitaeidi

Melitaea athalia	*heath fritillary*
M. cinxia	*Glanville fritillary*
Euphydryas aurinia	*marsh fritillary*

*Left: High brown fritillary **Argynnis cydippe**.*
*Top: Mountain species **Melitaea didyma**.*
Centre: Pearl-bordered fritillaries mating.
*Bottom: Small pearl-bordered **Clossiana selene**.*

Frogmouth

Frogmouths are birds related to the nightjar, and are named for their wide mouths that open in a frog-like gape. There are 12 species, ranging in length from 9 to 21 in. Their plumage is soft and silky and is patterned with streaks and bars, so they resemble owls in size, softness of plumage and general colouring. Frogmouths have two basic body colours: greyish and red-brown, being either one or the other, regardless of species. This is known as dichromatism.

Frogmouths live in the tropical forests and bush country of southeast Asia and in Australia. They are found from India to the Solomon Islands. The large tawny frogmouth, or mopoke, is found in most of Australia and on Tasmania. Recently one species has been found in Yunnan, southern China.

Silent night flier

Like their relatives the nightjars and oil-birds, frogmouths are nocturnal, which has made study of their habits difficult. They are active mainly after dusk and before dawn, but their calls may be heard throughout the night. The call of the mopoke is a muffled 'oom-oom'. Frogmouths are seen singly or in pairs, and are nowhere abundant. They are fast fliers but are not as agile as the nightjars; but their flight is silent for their wing feathers are downy, like those of owls.

Luring or hunting?

At one time the frogmouths' method of feeding was a matter of speculation, as no one had actually watched them. Because they had such large mouths, it was suggested that they hawked insects, flying about after moths and beetles with their mouths agape, like living butterfly nets. This idea was supported by the rictal bristles around the mouth. In other insect-eating birds these are used to increase the area of the 'net'. Another, bizarre suggestion was that frogmouths sat on branches with their beaks open, revealing pink or yellow mouths. Insects were attracted under the impression that these were brightly-coloured flowers and therefore a source of nectar.

In fact, frogmouths employ neither of these methods. They catch their prey when it is motionless or only moving slowly. Some frogmouths wait on a perch and drop to the ground to catch an insect, while others fly around trees and bushes picking insects off leaves or branches. Insects are their main food, but they also catch centipedes, scorpions, snails, frogs and even small mammals and birds.

Loose, flimsy nests

Most of our knowledge of the frogmouths' breeding habits comes from studies in captivity. The nests are flimsy. Some frogmouths build a nest of twigs in a horizontal fork of a branch. The twigs are woven so loosely that the 2 or 3 eggs can often be seen from below. Other frogmouths make a pad of their own down, bound with spiders' webs and camouflaged with lichen. Some reports suggest that only the female incubates the eggs, or that the female incubates at night and the male by day, but the male was the only one to incubate in a pair of tawny frogmouths kept in a zoo. After about 30 days the chicks hatch, clad in white down. Both parents share in feeding them. Feathers start to appear after a week.

The tawny frogmouth is one of the birds that has been reported to carry young on its back. AH Chisholm recounts how a young frogmouth that had left its nest, but was unable to fly, was disturbed by a small boy. One of its parents flew to the youngster, which climbed on its back and was carried away from danger. If a frogmouth is disturbed while on the nest its reaction is bluff rather than threat. It lowers its wings and raises the feathers around its head, so it looks much larger. At the same time it opens its mouth and 'glowers' at the intruder, a sight no doubt scaring enough to deter all but the boldest of enemies.

Out on a limb

If disturbed at night away from its nest, a frogmouth will fly away. During the day, however, it will 'freeze' on its perch on the limb of a tree with its bill pointed towards the sky. With its plumage greyish or reddish-brown with dark markings, the frogmouth looks for all the world like the broken stub of a branch. Indeed, this is very necessary for an animal that sleeps in the open during the day. So still are the frogmouths that at one zoo a notice reading 'This bird is alive' had to be put on their aviary to forestall repeated questions from the public, while the famous ornithologist Gould found that he could shoot one frogmouth without disturbing another perching beside it.

class	**Aves**
order	**Caprimulgiformes**
family	**Podargidae**
genera	***Batrochostomus*** ***Podargus***

John Markham

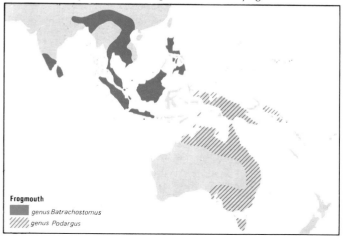

Graham Pizzey: Photo Res.

◁ *Bluff by tawny frogmouth* **P. strigoides** △ *Marbled frogmouth* **P. ocellatus**

Frogmouth
▓ *genus Batrachostomus*
▨ *genus Podargus*

Fruit bat

There are 160 species of fruit bats; 60 of these are known as flying foxes (see p. 947) and not all eat fruit, so their common name can be misleading. Scientifically, they are known as the Megachiroptera — literally 'big bats' — although some are small.

The Megachiroptera differ from the Microchiroptera (small or insect-eating bats) in a number of important ways. Their build is much the same as in the insect-eating bats: 4 fingers on each hand are greatly elongated and these, with the long forearm, form the main support for the web of skin, or wing membrane, used in flying. The fingers have the same number of bones as ours but each is very much longer. All bats have the first digit (thumb) free of the wing membrane and this has a claw which, with the claws of the hind feet, is used in climbing. Fruit bats differ in that the second finger ends in a claw, which is never found in insect-eating bats. Another difference is that fruit bats either have no tail, or only a stump. As a result they either have no tail membrane (or only a small one) whereas in the insect-eating bats the wing membrane, after joining the hindlegs, is continued to the tail, and this tail membrane is used as a pouch for the temporary storage of food.

Tongue-clicking bats

The head and face of a fruit bat is less grotesque than that of most insect-eating bats because there is no earlet, or tragus, in the ear, and because no fruit bat carries the folds of skin on the face, known as nose-leaves, used in echolocation. Fruit bats rely mainly on sight, but some of them use a simple form of echolocation. They listen for the echoes from clicks of the tongue instead of high-pitched squeaks.

There are no fruit bats in the New World, and in the Old World they are confined mainly to the tropics, especially where heavy rains give a profusion of trees: in Africa, India, southeast Asia and northern Australia. The short-eared fruit bat *Cynopterus sphinx,* the common bat of the Far East, weighs 1 oz but will eat 2 oz of ripe banana in 3 hours. It also frequently drinks nectar from trees whose blossoms open at night. The bat thrusts its head in to reach the nectar, its head becomes covered with pollen and when it visits the next flower it pollinates it. Its relative *C. brachyotis* in Ceylon roosts in the umbrella-like leaves of the talipot palm, 6–12 to a tree. Each hangs from the midrib of a frond by one foot with its wings wrapped around its body. Sometimes small companies will bite out the centres of the fruit clusters of the kitul palm, leaving a hollow in which they roost.

Tree-roosting fruit bats in a Nigerian forest hang in heavy clusters from every branch. They often quit areas where fruit is not available, commuting between roosting and feeding areas.

Peter Ward

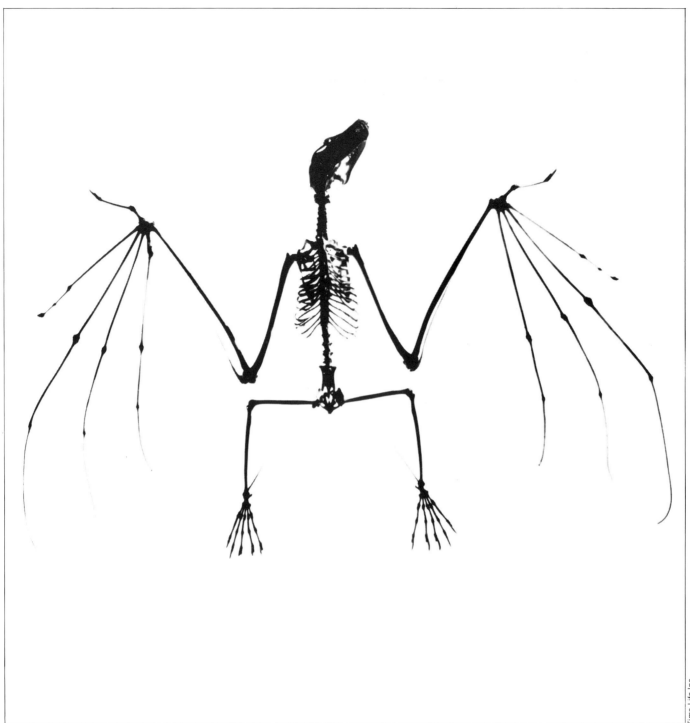

Time Life Inc.

Ten thousand calls an evening

Epauletted bats are common throughout the savannahs and forests of West Africa. They range from pygmies only 3 in. long to giants with a wingspan of 2½ ft. Their fur and wings are buff or brown, with small tufts of pure white at the base of each ear. The males have epaulettes of long silky white hairs tucked away in reversible pockets on their shoulders. These can be turned inside-out to show the white epaulette, for what reason is not clear. All have disproportionately large heads with dog-like faces. They feed mainly on fruits and the nectar and petals of flowers. Sometimes the food is eaten where it is picked, but usually the bat stuffs its cheek pouches and flies to a convenient perch to eat. It does not swallow the fruit but works a mouthful backwards and forwards from one cheek pouch to another, chewing it with its large sharp teeth until it has extracted all the juices. These it swallows, spitting out a pellet of fibres. Where epauletted bats have been feeding, the ground under the trees is carpeted with such pellets. At night, when feeding, they make a loud chewing noise. In addition the males are extremely vocal. Observations have been made on the noisy calling of Franquet's fruit bat *Epomops franqueti*. The males hang up in favourite trees, each in its territory, about 100 yd apart. From a distance of a mile their calling sounds rather like a flock of excited jackdaws. Close to, the individual males sound like cracked sheep-bells. One began calling at about 19 15 hours each evening and continued until 22 00 hours. His calls averaged 60 to the minute, which meant that in a single evening he gave nearly 10 000 calls. Then he was quiet until some time before dawn when he started up again and continued piping until first light.

The hammerheaded bat *Hypsignathus monstrosus* of West and Central Africa is 10½ in. long and has a wingspan of 3 ft. It has a large head with a swollen face, pendulous upper lip and a split lower lip. It is the noisiest of all bats and it has a bony voice-box which fills ⅓ of the body cavity, pushing the heart and lungs backwards and sideways. There are two hollow sacs beside the voice-box which act as resonators. Males and females occupy separate roosts and the

Jane Burton: Photo Res.

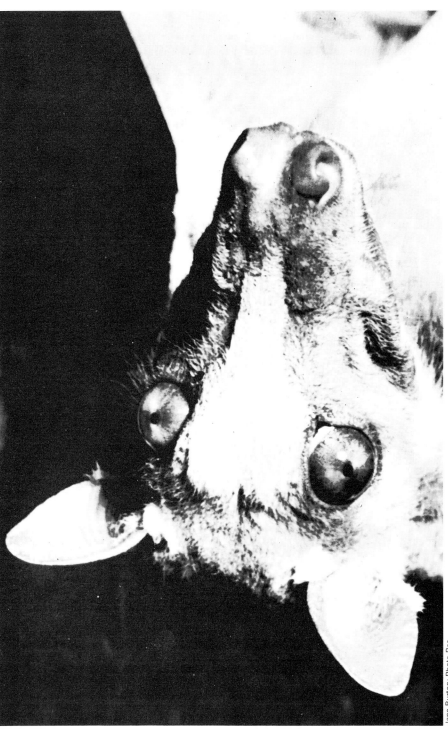

Jane Burton: Photo Res.

◁ *Fruit bat skeleton shows the long, elongated skull—much more pointed than in other bats. Notice how the basic mammal's skeleton has been modified so that the five fingers are prolonged into the 'umbrella-ribs' supporting the bat's flying membrane.*

△ *Caught in the act:* **Artibeus jamaicensis** *in the latter stages of gorging itself on a ripe pawpaw in Barbados. This is not a true fruit bat but one of the microchiroptera that has taken to eating fruit. Each mouthful is chewed until the juice is squeezed out and swallowed, then a pellet of drained fibres is spat out. Unlike most animals, but in common with man and guinea pigs, fruit bats cannot make vitamin C which they get from fruit.*

▷ *That upside-down feeling: a resting fruit bat* **Hypsignathus monstrosus** *squinnies at camera.*

young of both sexes are in a separate roost. From 18 15 – 23 00 hours the males call every half-second. The chorus is resumed for a while before dawn. This constant repetition of a loud, explosive 'kwok' could be territorial or to attract the females, except that the females seem to take no notice and the males crowd together in one tree to chorus.

The straw-coloured bat *Eidolon helvum* is the best known of the smaller fruit bats. It is found all over Africa south of the Sahara and is noted for its nomadic habits. Its wingspan is 2½ ft and it moves in groups of 1 000 or more from one ripening fruit crop to another. These groups are often attacked by local inhabitants, to be cooked and eaten. The straw-coloured bat chews fruit but swallows only the juice, the solid part being

spat out. The Arabian straw-coloured bat *E. sabaeum* attacks the date crops which have to be protected while ripening with bags made of split and woven palm leaves. This bat has been known to bite into trunks of trees to lap up sap in times of drought.

'Humming bird' bats

The pollen-eating or long-tongued bats include some of the smallest fruit bats. They are 2 – 2½ in. long with long muzzles, long tongues and small teeth. They hover in front of night-blooming flowers, clinging for a moment to insert their slender heads and long tongues to take nectar and pollen. They are believed to help in pollination but in this as in most of their natural history we

are largely in the dark. Of the 17 species one lives in West Africa, the rest live on South Pacific islands, from New Guinea eastwards.

Slightly larger are the tube-nosed bats, with 12 species in the area from Malaya to northern Australia. Their nostrils are at the ends of long tubes. When the bats call with a high whistling note the tubular nostrils move with a trembling motion. It is believed they are concerned with echo-location but proof of this is still needed.

class	**Mammalia**
order	**Chiroptera**
suborder	**Megachiroptera**
family	**Pteropidae**

981

Fruit fly

Fruit flies are very small insects that go almost unnoticed unless they have to be fished out of a drink, but they are one of the most important laboratory animals. Fruit flies are true flies, with club-shaped halteres (modified vestigial wings) instead of a rear pair of wings. Normal fruit flies are very much like houseflies in appearance, but only about ⅒ in. long. Their bodies are bulbous, yellowish or brownish in colour, and their eyes are red. They have a slow hovering flight with their abdomen hanging down, looking as if they are having difficulty in keeping airborne.

Vinegar flies and wine flies

Many of the different kinds of fruit fly are so similar that careful examination of minute features under a microscope is needed to tell them apart. About 2 000 species have been found, half of which live on Hawaii. For some reason there has been a massive evolution of fruit flies on

eggs are spindle-shaped with hair-like filaments at one end. The filaments may be used for breathing, as the eggs are often submerged in liquid with the filaments floating at the surface. The larvae have 11 segments each with a ring of hooked spines. At the rear is a telescopic organ bearing spiracles or breathing pores that can be raised above the liquid. The pupae breathe through feathery organs at the front end of the body.

With 2 000 or so species of fruit fly, many of which live in the same places and many having almost identical features, there must be some method by which species are prevented from interbreeding. Before mating, a male fruit fly courts the female, and she will only accept him if she is mature and of the same species. She recognises a male of the right species by sight, hearing or smell, or a combination of all three. The male fruit fly approaches the female, runs round her, licks her and finally mates. If they are of different species the female flies away, kicks the male or buzzes violently. While running around, the male vibrates one or both wings, and in some species it is the buzzing emitted by the wingbeats that is

attracted to light so they can easily be lured to one end of the container and transferred to another vessel without any being left behind or squashed. Their generation time is a fortnight; in other words the cycle of eggs, larvae, pupae and adults to the laying of the next generation of eggs takes a fortnight. This rapid breeding made them useful subjects for the study of population growth. If a pair of fruit flies are put into a milk bottle with food they start breeding and the population rises at an ever-increasing rate until a certain density is reached, when it slows down. Eventually the population levels off. The uneven growth rate, fast at first then slowing down, has been found in populations of many species from protozoa to man. The slowing-down has sometimes been found to be due to overcrowding. There is less food available for each individual and in fruit flies, as well as other animals, it has been found that females will not breed if they are constantly being disturbed.

Fruit flies have another and more important use. It was found that the cells of the salivary glands contained large chromosomes, and only two pairs of them. These are the string-like structures in the nucleus that carry the genetic information from one generation to another and which determine the hereditary characteristics of an individual. The large size of the fruit fly chromosomes made them very easy to study under the microscope. Moreover, as fruit flies bred very rapidly it was easy to study changes in the chromosomes, called mutations, and link them with corresponding changes in the bodies of the flies. One common change that occurs in fruit flies is for individuals to be hatched that have two pairs of wings instead of one pair of wings, and one pair of halteres. When body changes like this turn up, the chromosomes can be examined for changes in their structure. In this way a 'map' of the chromosomes can be made in which the pieces of genetical information, or genes, and the body character they control can be plotted. For instance, 100 genes have been found that control the eye shape.

These studies are helping us to understand the workings of heredity, and also the processes of evolution. Because of the rapid breeding rate it is possible to study the survival abilities of different forms of fruit flies, and so study the process of natural selection. Experiments have shown, for example, that light-coloured mutants do not survive as well in dry air as dark ones, but in wet air both types survive equally. Therefore, the two types live together in wet air, but if the humidity drops the dark fruit flies increase in number, replacing the light fruit flies.

Anthony Bannister: NHPA

*Colourful cousin: the Mediterranean fruit fly **Ceratitis capitata** is from the family Trypetidae.*

Hawaii. Perhaps they have been free to evolve in the isolation of the mid-Pacific in the same way as Darwin's finches (p. 751) evolved on the Galapagos Islands, only on a much larger scale. By contrast, there are 31 species in Britain, of which four are common. One arrived as recently as 1942, when it was found in London. It is now well established in the kitchens of restaurants and hospitals.

Fruit flies are also called vinegar flies or wine flies because they are attracted to weak solutions of acetic acid and alcohol, the principal ingredients of vinegar and wine respectively. They are often found in breweries, pickling plants, in bars and restaurants, where they settle on the rims of glasses and occasionally fall in. Fruit flies are also found in fruit stores where they feed on the juice, especially if it is fermenting. Other fruit flies feed on fungi or decaying plants or the sap flowing out of wounded plants.

Eggs submerged in liquid

The eggs, larvae and pupae of fruit flies live in the semi-liquid, often fermenting, substances that the adults feed on. The

important for identification of the species.

The buzzing is so faint that it has to be recorded by placing a fruit fly actually on the diaphragm of a microphone which is placed within several layers of soundproofing material. Even then it is necessary to make the recordings at night when all is quiet. All fruit flies of one species were found to buzz at the same frequency. The female is 'tuned in' to the frequency of her species, ignoring all others.

The female fruit fly lays batches of 15–20 white eggs each day, continuing until she has laid 400–900. When the larvae hatch, they burrow into the food material such as rotting fruit, staying there while they moult three times and emerging to pupate. The larvae of one species *Drosophila sigmoides* live in the froth of the cuckoo-spit insect rather than in rotting fruit.

Bred by the million

Fruit flies have been extensively used as laboratory animals because they breed very rapidly. They can be kept in milk bottles or other convenient containers and fed rotten bananas or other fruit. They are

phylum	**Arthropoda**
class	**Insecta**
order	**Diptera**
family	**Drosophilidae**
genus & species	***Drosophila melanogaster*** ***D. sigmoides*** ***D. simulans*** *others*

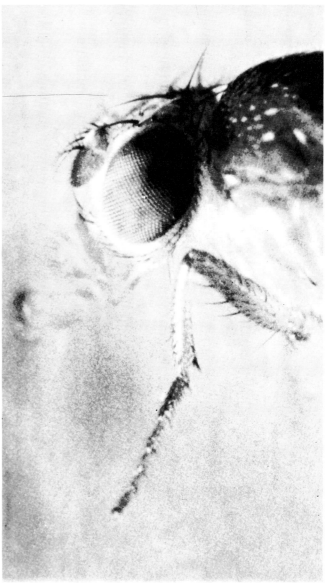

△ *In the mood: as many fruit fly species are alike, identification courtship precedes mating.*

▽ *Fruit flies mating. Their mutations and behaviour patterns are valuable to the scientist.*

△ *All-round vision: close-up showing the many facets of a fruit fly's compound eye.*

Photos by HC Bennet Clark and AW Ewing. University of Edinburgh

Fruit pigeon

The fruit pigeons are a large group of beautifully coloured pigeons which, although placed in one subfamily, are a varied group and may not be closely related to each other, there being five groups within the subfamily.

The green pigeons of Africa and southern Asia form a group of 20 species. They are pale yellow-green marked with yellow, orange, black or mauve. Another group is the imperial pigeons that range from Malaya through northern Australia and the Philippines to the islands of the South Pacific while the smaller and more brightly coloured fruit doves are found mainly in the South Pacific islands. Closely related to these are the topknot or flock pigeons of Australia and the blue fruit pigeons of the islands of the Indian Ocean.

Brilliant plumage, good camouflage

Fruit pigeons live mainly in the tropical

New Zealand fruit pigeon **Hemiphaga novaeseclandice**, *although colourful, is not conspicuous.*

forests of southeast Asia, Australia and the East Indies. A few spread east across the Pacific and west to Africa and some extend south to New Zealand and Tasmania. Fruit pigeons are not as gregarious as other pigeons; some live in fairly large flocks, but others live in pairs. Because tropical forests are inaccessible, the habits of many fruit pigeons are not well known, and very little is known of the fruit doves in particular. Despite their brilliant plumage, these pigeons are very well camouflaged, blending with the sun-dappled leaves so that even flocks of them pass unnoticed. Oliver Austin recounts in *Birds of the World* how on shooting one fruit dove that he had finally managed to spot, the rest of the flock which he had not seen flew out of the tree.

The other fruit pigeons also live in flocks, often high in the tall trees of the forests. They are nomadic, continually moving about in search of fruit. The yellow-bellied fruit pigeon of the East Indies feeds mainly on wild figs and moves about as the figs ripen in different places. As a result it may

be common in one place one year but not the next. Some species perform regular migrations rather than irregular movements. The Torres Strait or nutmeg pigeon, one of the imperial pigeons, migrates in flocks across the Torres Strait, from New Guinea to northern Queensland, where it breeds on the islands around the coast. From the islands it flies to the mainland every day to feed.

Leaving the pips

Fruit pigeons climb nimbly in search of fruits, berries and seeds – the African green pigeon will even hang upside down like a tit. Apart from fruits and seeds they find in the trees, a few fruit pigeons eat termites, rice or millet.

A feature of all fruit pigeons is their ability to open their bills wide to swallow fruit whole. The imperial pigeons have an unusually wide gape because their jaws have elastic sockets, like those of snakes. As a result, they can swallow fruit and nutmegs larger than their heads. The species that eat mainly fruit have a gizzard lined with hard ridges and lumps. Muscular action rubs the flesh of the fruit against the

gizzard wall so the soft flesh is torn off, the stones and pips passing straight through. The flesh is digested in the short, wide intestine. The fruit pigeons that eat seeds have a larger intestine, and a more muscular gizzard to crush them. Fig-eating fruit pigeons also have a muscular gizzard to crush the hundreds of small seeds in figs.

Openwork nests

Fruit pigeons make flimsy nests of twigs and rootlets. They are no more than a rough platform through which the eggs may be visible from below. The superb fruit pigeon builds a nest so flimsy that the sitting bird has to sit firm whenever the wind blows, holding the egg with her breast. The wedge-tailed fruit pigeon often nests near drongos (p. 806) to benefit from the ferocity with which these birds drive away enemies.

Incubation is carried out by the female, who is fed by the male. In the nutmeg pigeons the males make daily journeys from the islands to the mainland until the eggs hatch. Both parents feed the newly-hatched

young. All members of the pigeon family feed their young on pigeon's milk, a cheesy fluid, rich in protein and fats that is secreted from the lining of the crop. The adult fruit pigeon puts its head inside the mouth of the chick (the reverse of the usual procedure) and brings up the milk. After a few days the parents supplement the chicks' diet with fruit and seeds. The function of pigeon's milk seems to be to provide the young birds with a large amount of protein that they would not get from the adults' food. The fruit pigeons that eat mainly fruit lay one egg, whereas those that eat a lot of seeds lay two. This is probably because the fruit-eating pigeons cannot build up the reserves of protein necessary to lay two eggs or to feed two chicks on pigeon's milk.

Hunted for the pot

Throughout their range fruit pigeons are hunted for the pot and are said to be excellent eating. At one time it was thought that some might go the way of the recently extinct passenger pigeon that lived in North America in flocks of countless thousands. The early settlers in Australia used to slaughter nutmeg pigeons, and the flocks of 50–60 thousand were reduced to tens. The topknot pigeons were also reduced in numbers. These pigeons are now protected, although they are sometimes a nuisance when they attack fruit crops.

Brought to extinction

The island of Mauritius is famous for its extinct dodo. This is, however, only one of several animals that once lived on the island but succumbed to man's interference. The hackled pigeon once lived in countless numbers, but the last specimen was shot in 1826. This pigeon was also known as the pigeon hollandais, or Dutch pigeon, as its plumage of crimson, deep indigo and white recalled the Dutch flag with its horizontal stripes of red, white and blue.

The pigeon hollandais was killed off by the introduced Indian mynahs. Although so abundant the pigeon could not maintain its numbers against the depredations of the mynahs on its eggs and chicks. There are now only three specimens of the pigeon hollandais in existence in museums. Some may have been destroyed because it was not realised how valuable they were. In 1816 a French collection of 18 000 natural history specimens was bought by Edinburgh University. Not until 1855 was a specimen of the pigeon hollandais discovered in it.

Although the species is extinct, its name lives on. Another pigeon, living in Madagascar and the Seychelles, is called hollandais also because of its colouring.

class	**Aves**		
order	**Columbiformes**		
family	**Columbidae**		
subfamily	**Treroninae**		
genera	**Alectroenas** *blue fruit pigeons* **Ducula** *imperial pigeons* **Lopholaimus** *topknot pigeons* **Ptilinopus** *fruit doves* **Treron** *green pigeons*		

Fulmar

The fulmar's name is derived from 'foul-bird', based on its musky odour and its habit of spitting an evil-smelling oil at intruders. This habit is shared by many other members of the petrel family. The fulmar is a typical petrel: the body is short and stocky, 20 in. long, and the wings are long and narrow. In the north Atlantic the fulmar is silver grey above and whitish below, but in the Arctic Ocean and North Pacific many fulmars are a sooty brown, light on the undersides.

In the Southern Ocean there is a close relative of the fulmar, the silver-grey fulmar. It is slightly smaller than the fulmar but very similar in colour and habits. It breeds around Antarctica and on some sub-Antarctic islands.

Soaring in the updraughts

In flight, fulmars look like small albatrosses, gliding on outstretched wings over the sea, with only occasional wingbeats. Fulmars quarter the surface of the sea in search of food, but return to colonies on cliffs even outside the season during which they breed, where they can be seen soaring in the up-draughts, using their fanned tails as rudders. From a distance they can be mistaken for gulls, but their rapid wingbeats contrast with a gull's more leisurely flapping.

Over the last 100 years the fulmar has become a familiar sight in Britain. Up to 1878 the only known colony was on St Kilda, then in that year a dozen pairs were found breeding on the Kame, a 1 200-ft cliff on the Shetland island of Foula. Since then fulmars have spread around the British Isles as far as the south coast, and the new colonies are increasing in numbers. On Foula, for instance, the numbers rose to about 4 000 pairs by 1966 and they now breed inland, on rocky faces and in abandoned crofter's cottages and stone walls.

The increase has not been restricted to Britain. There have been remarkable increases in fulmar populations in Iceland and the Faeroes, starting in the former about 1710 and in the Faeroes about 1810. In all three places the increase seems to have started from a few restricted colonies and new colonies have formed from these in a progressive spread around the coasts.

One reason suggested for the vast increase in fulmars, now among the commonest birds in the North Atlantic, is that first the Arctic whaling industry then the opening up of fishing grounds around Iceland, the Faeroes and the British Isles have provided fulmars with an almost limitless supply of food. Whenever a whale was being cut up for its blubber, fulmars gathered in their thousands to feed on the pieces of blubber and flesh. Nowadays they gather to feed on fish offal thrown over from trawlers.

Surface feeders

Fulmars feed on the surface of the water, dipping their heads in or occasionally up-ending like ducks. They mainly feed on squid, fish such as sand-eels and young herrings and crustaceans, but will also take jellyfish, comb jellies and other animals that live at the surface of the sea. The feeding on man-made supplies of food is probably a development of the fulmars' habit of feeding on dead seals, walruses and whales in the Arctic or on the carcasses of birds.

Fulmars on the rocks: nesting on cliffs gives them protection against many would-be predators.

G Rüppell

Winter courtship

The breeding colonies are visited in winter; the fulmars courting from December to February onwards. Pairs of fulmars sit together on their nest sites cackling rather like domestic chickens. At the same time they nibble the plumage of their partner's head and fence with their bills. The single white egg is laid either on bare rock or in a slight depression in the soil made by the female. Nest sites are on small rocky ledges or crevices in cliffs or — where the fulmars are not disturbed — on flat ground, especially in abandoned buildings or by stone walls. In the British Isles it is rare to find fulmar nests far from cliff tops, but in Spitzbergen they have been found nesting 20 miles inland.

In the British Isles most of the eggs are laid in late May, but nearly a month later in the Arctic. Just before laying the fulmars leave the nest site for about a fortnight and disappear out to sea. It is thought that this pre-laying exodus or honeymoon, as it is variously called, enables the birds to put on weight. This is necessary, for egg laying takes a fair proportion of the females' food reserves, while the male has to fast for a week while he takes the first stint of incubation.

The chicks hatch after 40–50 days' incubation. At first they are covered with a white, fluffy down. They spend 7–8 weeks at the nest site before flying. Both adults feed the chick. As the chick spits oil at everything that comes near it, the parent has to alight near the nest and cackle until the chick recognises it and sets up a regular monotonous call with which it solicits food. The adult fulmar then regurgitates half-digested food which the chick takes from its bill.

Cliff-hanging for safety

Fulmars are preyed on by bald eagles, gulls and skuas, which take adults, chicks and abandoned eggs. To some extent, at least, the fulmars' ability to spit oil seems to be an effective deterrent against their enemies. The chicks can spit several times in succession, each jet travelling 3 or 4 ft. The aim is not always very good, but is sufficient to hit any intruder at the entrance to a nest crevice.

Nesting on cliffs is undoubtedly a protection against many enemies. Mammals such as Arctic foxes are completely deterred. Flesh-eating birds can get to the cliff ledges, but if these are narrow they will have difficulty in landing to catch their prey. In the North Atlantic, however, man has made a habit of collecting cliff-nesting birds and their eggs for food. In parts of Shetland, for instance, each man had a section of cliff which he alone could harvest. On St Kilda, until its human occupants were evacuated in 1930, the community was the only one in the British Isles to rely mainly on birds' flesh for protein. The St Kildans worked the cliffs in teams for fulmars and the catch was divided between the men in each team. Their feats of rock climbing were prodigious, as were those of the islanders of Shetland, Faeroe, Iceland and Greenland. In the latter two countries, large numbers of fulmars were taken for their flesh, oil and feathers, until several people had contracted psittacosis or parrot-virus and in 1940 it was shown that fulmars carried the disease.

Oily deterrent

The oil-spitting habit of the fulmar is never forgotten by anyone who has climbed around the cliffs in search of them or who has walked beside a dry stone wall and failed to retreat at the first 'f-chee' as a fulmar chick heralds its presence. On the islands around the Antarctic, the cliffs similarly abound with cape pigeons and snow petrels which also have the habit of spitting defiance and oil at intruders.

It is a foul liquid, often amber in colour, warm, sticky and smelling very strongly of cod-liver oil. The chicks generally spit farther, more accurately and more consistently than their parents. Their aim often goes wild but many a bird watcher has frantically rubbed oil from his face or camera lens. Cautious men have taken rash steps on cliffs to avoid fulmar nests and

986

G Rüppell

many bird ringers have found their clothes unwearable except in strictest solitude. The oil comes from the stomach which is larger in petrels than in most other birds. Analysis has shown that the oil from the stomachs of petrels and albatrosses is a mixture of waxes, fatty acids and hydrocarbons and comes from their food.

While oil spitting is undoubtedly used in defence, and peregrines have been recorded as being fouled with fulmar oil, the primary function of the oil is to provide the chicks with rich, semi-digested food. Petrels feed far out to sea and they can bring more food to the chicks if its bulk is reduced by partial digestion and the removal of water. It is common for birds to gape and lunge at intruders at the nest, and the two habits may have become combined in the fulmar and its relatives.

△ *Landing approach: three successive stages in a fulmar's flight attitude, with the wings being flexed to decrease the bird's forward speed and its 'undercarriage' being lowered at right, with wings spread again for a final halt.*

▷ *Suspicious glance from a fulmar, showing the distinctive tube-shaped nostril cover found in all petrels. This 'tubenose' arrangement may be to help the nasal gland to excrete salt, or an extension of the highly-developed sense of smell.*

Eric Hosking

class	**Aves**
order	**Procellariiformes**
family	**Procellariidae**
genus & species	***Fulmarus glacialis*** *fulmar* *F. glacialoides* *silver-grey fulmar*

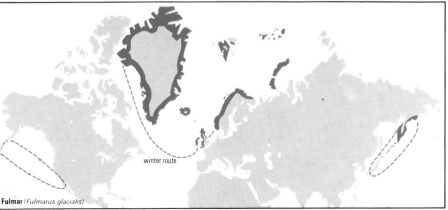

winter route

Fulmar (*Fulmarus glacialis*)

Fur seal

The fur seal was once known better to most people as a fur coat than as a marine mammal. Over the past 200 years or so many thousands have been slaughtered by hunters, and the animals have been brought to the verge of extinction. One species lives in the northern hemisphere, and six species in the southern.

The northern fur seal is larger than its southern counterpart. Adult males grow to 8 ft long and weigh 600 lb, the females being just over 5 ft long and up to 130 lb weight. This considerable difference in size between the sexes is common among seals. The southern seals grow to just over 6 ft and weigh up to 350 lb (males) and 4½ ft to just over 100 lb (females).

The fur seals belong to the family Otariidae, or eared seals. That is they have a small external ear, not found in the Phocidae or true seals. Other distinguishing features are the ability to turn the hindflippers forward and walk with the body raised from the ground, as well as having the body covered with a dense fur quite unlike the coarse hairs of the phocid seals. The foreflippers are large and mobile. The hindflippers have small nails used in grooming, the animal being able to reach its face and neck with the hindflipper.

Adult seals vary considerably in colour depending on whether they are wet or dry; a wet female may look almost entirely silver, but dries a dark brown. The males show less of a change, looking black when wet and also drying to a dark brown. In both sexes the underside is paler. The flippers are hairless, dark brown, and leathery. Young animals of both sexes are more the colour of adult females and may easily be confused with them.

Seals have ticklish whiskers

Seals spend much of their time in water but they also haul out onto beaches to rest. It was noticed by people working among the southern fur seals that they are decidedly ticklish. The beaches are often crowded and anyone moving among the seals needs some form of protection. He

△ In the nursery: a fur seal toddler surveys its torpid playmates and elders.

RW Vaughan

△ An adult colony poses on the rocks.

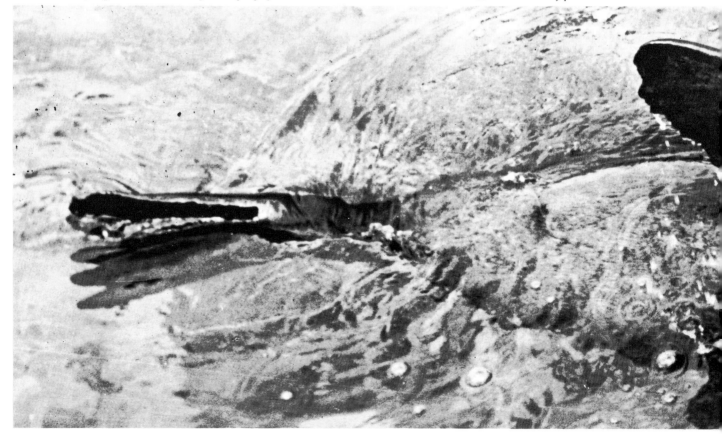

usually carries a light bamboo pole to fend off angry seals, but it is useless to belabour them around the head or body. This only annoys them more whereas a gentle tickling of the whiskers will nearly always cause the seal to move aside. This sensitivity of the whiskers is made use of by the cows when they are disturbed by bulls on the breeding beaches. They snap at his whiskers, so driving him away. If he is particularly persistent she may even hang onto his whiskers or bite at his chest. Possibly these sensitive whiskers are used in feeding, as organs of touch, especially when the animal is feeding on the sea bottom, or in murky waters.

Strange food facts

The northern fur seal eats mostly fish, such as herring and pollack, but it also takes squid. It has been blamed by the canners for taking Pacific salmon, but whether it harms the industry has yet to be proved. One fur seal made history when a new species of deepsea fish *Bathylagus callorhinus* was found in its stomach. This also showed that fur seals sometimes dive very deep to catch their food. The southern species seems to exist to a large extent on krill, a small crustacean particularly abundant in Antarctic waters which forms the staple diet of whales and penguins as well as seals.

Competition for mates

The six species of southern fur seal differ slightly in the pattern of their breeding, but that of the Kerguelen fur seal, also found in large numbers at South Georgia, is fairly typical. In late September or early October the breeding season begins when the first bulls come ashore to take up territories, but it is not until late October that the beaches begin to fill up. There is then a certain amount of territorial fighting as the bulls divide up the beach among themselves. Sometimes violent fights take place with the bulls taking each other by the scruff of the neck and shaking each other violently, occasionally causing quite serious-looking injuries. By early November the first cows arrive on the beaches and the bulls patrol up and down their territories trying to keep the females from straying. As the number of females on the beach increases, each bull has a harder task trying to keep his group of cows or harem together. The younger bulls, unable to gain a proper territory on the beach, occupy a piece of tidal strip or land well to the back of the beach. Some may even be able to hold a little territory of their own with perhaps one female. About 2 or 3 days

Northern fur seal
■ *Callorhinus ursinus*
Southern fur seals
Arctocephalus pusillus
A. forsteri
A. doriferus
A. tropicalis
A. australis
A. philippii

WLN Tickell

▽ *Fur seal back-stroke: casual male waves a languid flipper.*

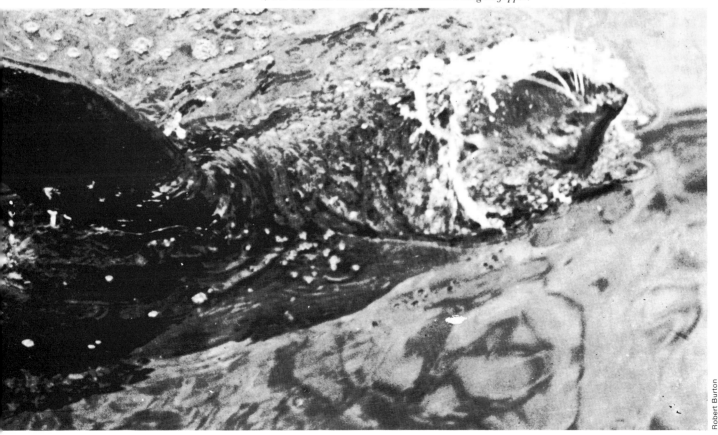

Robert Burton

after coming ashore the cows give birth to their pups. In the southern fur seals the pups are 1½ ft long and weigh about 10 lb at birth; those of the northern fur seal are 2½ ft and 14 lb. In all species they are covered in black woolly hair which is moulted after 6 or 7 weeks. The pups are suckled for up to 3 months, but after the first few days the cow leaves her pup at intervals to go to sea and feed, returning every few days to suckle it. After about a week the cow mates with the bull and so the whole cycle is started again. The pattern is much the same for the northern fur seal except that the bulls come ashore in June. Female seals reach adult size in 3 years, males in 6—7 years. Fur seals probably live for 30 years but do not breed beyond 20 years of age.

◁ *Fur seal nursery off southern Australia.*

△ *Look of appeal: a youngster on a snowy beach.*

WLN Tickell

Beset by dangers

The most natural enemy of seals is the killer whale, which kills mainly the younger animals but also takes adults. Occasionally seals are seen with a flipper missing, or with other serious injuries, almost certainly caused by killer whales. There is a record of a killer whale being found with the remains of 24 fur seals in its stomach. Young pups of the southern species may be molested by giant petrels. Parasites are often found in fur seals, one of the most important being the hookworm. This causes a high mortality among the northern fur seal pups, and in 1948 biologists found over 20 000 dead pups along 1½ miles of beach in the Pribilof Islands, many of which had died from hookworm infection. Some pups die

because of overcrowding on the beaches, being trampled to death, especially by the bulls during territorial disputes. Above all, man is probably the greatest enemy, although he is less so today than in the past.

The brink of extinction

The northern or Pribilof fur seals were discovered towards the end of the 18th century by the Russian explorer Pribilof. At that time the herds numbered about 2½ million but hunting reduced this to about 200 000 in the early part of this century. In 1911 an agreement was made between Russia, America and Japan to limit the numbers of seals hunted at sea, and the herds have increased · in size as a result of this protection. At the present time there is a carefully controlled industry taking about 60 000 animals each year, only the younger males in the 4—6 age group being taken as these not only make the best pelts but also the males are surplus to the breeding requirements of the herd as will be seen below.

The southern fur seals were discovered by Captain Cook at the time of his voyage in 1775. His reports of huge numbers of sea-bears soon caused a rush of sealers to the Antarctic, the Americans being particularly prominent, and around 1800 the herds were very heavily hunted. It was calculated by Weddell that at least 1 200 000 skins had been taken from South Georgia itself by 1822, and he noted that the seals were almost extinct at this date. Other colonies around the Antarctic were also being fully exploited at this time, hunters

working at the Falkland Islands, South Shetlands and around Cape Horn, the last region being where the sealers first found fur seals in the 1780s.

International seal conservation

The great slaughter that went on in both northern and southern hemispheres caused such devastation because the sealers were in the habit of killing all the seals they could lay their hands on, male, female or pups, regardless of the quality of their pelts. Twice in the 50 years after the discovery of the Pribilof herds the seals were almost exterminated, but each time they recovered only to be hunted down again. Eventually international agreement on the killing allowed the herds to be built up again, and during the last 50 years they have been the subject of an intensive scientific study, and their management is very strictly controlled by the United States Government. Only the young males are taken and these are carefully driven from the colony into corrals and suitable animals selected for killing, the remainder being allowed to return to the beaches.

The skins are taken off, the blubber is removed and the pelts salted. They are then shipped to the processing plant where the longer, coarse guard hairs are removed leaving the fine underfur, which must be straightened and dyed. This process takes about 3 months. The pelts are graded and finally sent away to be auctioned and turned into coats and other articles of fashion.

The story of the southern seals is similar but here the sealers seemed to be particularly thorough and there was no government protection at first. The seals were almost totally exterminated and for a long period at the end of the 19th century the sealers found no fur seals and had to be content with oil from elephant seals and penguins. There appear to have been only a handful of animals left at the beginning of this century, and for about forty years only very small groups were seen. But during the last 20 years fur seals have been found in increasing numbers in the Antarctic, and their numbers have now increased quite dramatically. The distribution of southern fur seals at the present time extends from South America, the Falkland Islands, South Georgia, South Sandwich Islands, Australia, Tasmania, New Zealand, South Africa, Kerguelen, to most of the sub-Antarctic islands.

class	**Mammalia**
order	**Pinnipedia**
family	**Otariidae**
genera & species	***Callorhinus ursinus*** *northern* ***Arctocephalus pusillus*** *South Africa* *others*

Gallinule

Gallinules are relatives of the coots and crakes, belonging to two genera: **Porphyrio**, *the purple gallinule or swamp hen, and* **Porphyrula**, *the American gallinule. They are closely related to the moorhen, which is called the common gallinule in North America. Like coots, gallinules have frontal shields rising from the base of the bill. The plumage is a purple-black, with brown on the upper parts. The legs and toes are long and the feet are not webbed.*

The purple gallinule is very widespread, ranging from southern Europe east and south to New Zealand and the Chatham Islands, and from open steppe to tropical rain forests. At one time it must have been a very flourishing species as until a short time ago it was found in isolated islands such as Mauritius and Reunion, as well as New Zealand and the Chatham Islands. It was once common in southern Europe, where, with the crested coot, it spread from Africa as a rather exotic addition to the fauna. The spoiling of its habitat by human activities (mainly draining of wet lands) has now made it rare in Europe. It can still be found in Sicily, in wild parts of Spain such as the Coto Doñana and it may still linger on in southern France. The American gallinule ranges from the southern United States to northern Argentina, including the West Indies.

Damp habitat

Like most of the rail family, the gallinules live near water, among dense water plants surrounding lakes, pools, streams and marshes. Their long toes enable them to walk about on the leaves of lilies and other plants growing on the surface of the water. They are shy birds but can be seen wending their way through the tangled vegetation, flicking their tails at every step like coots or moorhens. Gallinules swim well and frequently climb trees where they may roost at night.

A wide-ranging diet

Gallinules feed on plants and animals. They eat flowers and waterplant leaves and will climb trees to eat berries such as mulberries, while waterplants and the bottom of shallow water are searched for molluscs, crustaceans and other small animals. The study of what gallinules eat is sometimes made easy by their habit of building feeding platforms of plants, which become littered with the remains of their meals. It is not known whether all gallinules build feeding platforms, but the purple gallinule of southern Spain and western Australia (where it is known as the western swamp hen) are known to do so. They often eat tadpoles and aquatic insects; the remains of snail shells are often found on the feeding platforms and bloodstains show that they eat leeches. In southern Spain gallinules have been known to eat water snakes.

Nests with runways

Outside the breeding season gallinules live in flocks and in some parts of their range they are migratory. In the southern United States pairs start to form shortly after arrival in the spring, or even while en route. Each pair defends a territory about 200 ft along the bank of a stream or pool. Within this territory the birds feed separately, keeping in contact with one another by calling continually. They display to each other with their white tail feathers or by bowing with neck outstretched and wings held out from the body.

A couple of weeks after the start of courtship, the nest is built. This is made of plants piled upon each other, sometimes floating in deep water and sometimes built on the bed in shallow water. The plants are woven into the standing stems of water plants, both anchoring and camouflaging the nest.

Gaudy coot relative, a purple gallinule moodily straddles its toes in the shallows.

The nest is about 10 in. across and as much as 20 in. high, with a cup at the top 2–3 in. deep. A peculiar feature is a runway 2–4 in. wide that leads at a steep angle up to the nest. Sometimes the runway, made of piled up plants, may go for 10 ft or so through the surrounding vegetation and is used by the parent gallinules for leaving the nest unobtrusively when danger threatens.

Up to 7 eggs are laid and incubated for about 22 days. Both parents sit on the eggs, taking turns of 3–4 hours each. When a gallinule arrives to take a spell on the nest it often brings a piece of a plant which it presents to its mate. This is not an uncommon feature of courtship in birds which the gallinule carries on into the nesting period. The chicks leave the nest shortly after hatching but will return to roost, climbing up the runway, using their wings to help pull themselves up. Both parents bring food to the chicks, giving them mainly insects and other arthropods.

Slaughtered by pesticide

In 1949 a project was set up in the Wageningen district of Surinam to grow rice on a large scale using mechanised rather than traditional methods. A large area of swamp was cleared and intensive rice-growing started. Not surprisingly in this tropical region the crops attracted a large number of pests, from rats to snails. One of these pests was the gallinule. Although they feed on freshwater animals and so might be considered to have a useful controlling influence, they also feed on plants to some extent. They really became a nuisance, however, when they gathered in non-breeding flocks and broke the rice plants by attempting to perch on them. The solution to this was to poison the flocks. Endrin, a pesticide, so powerful that it is banned in some countries, was sprayed from low-flying aircraft early in the morning as the gallinules sat on the rice. Such treatment is rather drastic and it is surprising that any pest of any kind survived. Probably the only pest-control programme to beat this is the use of dynamite to kill weaverbirds in Africa.

class	**Aves**
order	**Gruiformes**
family	**Rallidae**
genera & species	***Porphyrio porphyrio*** *purple gallinule* ***Porphyrula martinica*** *American gallinule others*

Arthur Christiansen

Gall wasp

The familiar oak apples and marble galls on oak, and 'robin's pin-cushion' on wild roses are made by insect larvae. Some of these are made by the gall wasps, minute insects belonging to the order Hymenoptera and forming a superfamily, the Cynipoidea. They are closely related to the chalcid wasps (p. 544). Over 80% of cynipid wasps make their galls on oak and about 7% of them affect roses. There are 228 species of cynipid wasps in Britain alone. Other gall-forming insects include certain saw-flies (also Hymenoptera), the gall flies and gall midges (Diptera) and some of the aphids (Hemiptera). In most cases, as in gall wasps, particular species confine their attentions to one species or genus of plant.

Food and shelter for the larvae

All gall wasps lay their eggs in the tissues of some particular part of the plant, a flower-bud, a leaf-bud, the blade of a leaf or even the root. No effect is seen until the minute larva hatches from the egg, but from this time on, the tissue of the plant surrounding the larva develops abnormally, usually swelling up and providing the insect with both shelter and food. It is believed that the plant tissues are stimulated to grow in this irregular way by some secretion given out by the larva. The swelling size, colour and shape of the gall depend on the species of wasp that laid the egg. In some cases a number of eggs are laid and the larvae grow up together enclosed in the same gall. The activities of the mature insects, as far as they are known, seem to be concerned almost solely with completing the complicated life cycles typical of gall wasps.

Types of gall

There are many different types of gall only a few of which can be described here.

Oak apple. When fully formed the oak apple is a round, spongy, fruit-like object, 1–2 in. diameter and coloured light brown or pink. If opened in June and July when mature it will be found to contain a number of larvae, usually about 30, each enclosed in a little chamber in the gall tissue. The oak apple represents a stage in the life history of the gall wasp *Biorhiza pallida*, whose life cycle will be described later.

Marble gall. Caused by the gall wasp *Andricus kollari*, this is the most familiar of all the oak galls and is often mis-named 'oak apple'. It is green when it reaches full growth—rather less than 1 in. diameter—in August and then turns brown and woody and remains on the twig after the leaves fall, when it is very conspicuous. It harbours only one larva of the gall wasp, whose exit hole can be seen in an old gall. Often there is more than one exit hole, and this means that the gall has harboured other parasites or 'inquilines'. Males of this gall wasp are quite unknown. In an attempt to find them 1½ bushels of the galls were once collected and the wasps bred out, but among over 12 000 females that hatched not one male was found.

Common spangle gall. In July numbers of little round button-like objects can often be seen on the undersides of oak leaves, attached by a central stalk, so they look like tiny, very short-stemmed mushrooms. This is one of the two kinds of gall formed by *Neuroterus quercus-baccarum.* Each contains a single larva, and in September the stems break, and the galls fall to the ground where the insects inside them pass the winter. The wasps that hatch in April (females only) climb the trees again and give rise to currant galls, which look like bunches of red currants and in no way resemble the spangle galls, which the next generation of wasps will again produce. This alternation of generations is more fully described below.

Bedeguar gall. Also known as the moss gall or robin's pin-cushion this spectacular gall of wild rose bushes is almost as familiar as the marble gall. The part containing the larvae is surrounded by a tangled mass of branched fibres, green at first, turning to bright red in July and August. Inside it are 50 or more cells, each containing a larva of the gall wasp *Diplolepis rosae.*

Unusual life history

In many gall wasps there is an 'alternation

*Top left: Spangle galls on underside of leaf.
Top right: Marble gall showing exit hole, with oak apple sectioned to show grub. Above:
Ready to face the world, a wasp leaves its gall.*

of generations', already mentioned in connection with the spangle and currant galls. The rather similar life cycle of the oak apple gall wasp *Biorhiza pallida* shows this.

When the oak apple is mature, the larvae in it pupate; the wasps hatch in July and eat their way out. They include both males and females, the former being winged, the latter wingless. After mating, the females crawl down the trunk of the tree and enter the soil, making their way to the small fibrous roots, in which they lay their eggs. When the larvae hatch, galls develop on the roots, round, dark brown and of ½ in. diameter, wholly unlike an oak apple. The wasps which emerge from these are all wingless females. They must find the tree trunk, crawl up it and seek the ends of the shoots, where they lay their eggs (without mating) in the terminal buds. When these hatch the larvae form a new generation of oak apples.

In the case of the spangle gall and currant gall wasp *Neuroterus quercus-baccarum* the female-only generation appears in April,

993

having overwintered in the fallen spangle galls among dead leaves under the tree. These wasps lay unfertilised eggs which form the larvae, giving rise to the currant galls and causing a bi-sexual generation.

The life history of the marble gall wasp *Andricus kollari* is something of a mystery. We have mentioned that males of this gall wasp are quite unknown, but as long ago as 1882 an entomologist claimed that the species known as *Andricus circulans*, which makes galls on Turkey oak, is really the bi-sexual generation of *Andricus kollari*. This was confirmed in 1953.

Food always to hand

The sole food of the larva of any gall wasp is the substance of the gall which forms round it. The mature insects probably do little more than take a drink when needed.

Woodpeckers are known to peck open marble galls to get at the larva and currant galls are sometimes eaten by birds, which probably mistake them for fruit. By far the most serious enemies of gall wasps, however, are other insects which lay eggs in the gall. The larvae of some of these are parasites or predators on the 'legitimate' larva, the parasites slowly eating it alive, the predators

killing it and eating it outright. Others are inquilines, which feed on the substance of the gall, and so rob the primary inmate but do not otherwise harm it except sometimes to starve it enough to stunt its growth. The inquilines do not have it all their own way, for they too are preyed upon by predators and parasites, and these in their turn have parasites specially adapted to afflict them, known as hyperparasites. The inquilines are usually other species of gall wasp and the parasites chalcid wasps or ichneumons.

If bedeguar galls are collected in late winter and kept in jars over damp sand, a remarkable assembly of tiny wasps will emerge. In one such experiment only a quarter of the insects were *Diplolepis rosae*, the makers of the gall, and of these (which numbered over 16 000) less than 1% were males. No alternation of generations is known in *D. rosae*, and it looks as if males are on the way to disappearing altogether.

Make your own ink

The very common and familiar marble gall has been a feature of the British countryside only since 1834, when it was found in a nursery garden in Devon. The gall, with its

△ *Sliced-open gall shows a mature wasp and the chamber in which it has developed.*

wasp *Andricus kollari*, had been brought into the country for use in the dyeing industry and for making ink, the tannic acid in the galls being the chemical agent involved. In fact, anyone can make ink from marble galls. All you have to do is to bruise 4 oz of galls with a hammer, put them in a quart of boiling water and leave for 24 hours. Then take $1\frac{1}{2}$ oz of ferrous sulphate and dissolve rather less than an ounce of gum arabic in a little water. Filter the infusion of galls through cloth and add the other ingredients together with a few drops of carbolic acid. But perhaps it is better to buy a bottle of ink!

phylum	**Arthropoda**
class	**Insecta**
order	**Hymenoptera**
super-family	**Cynipoidea**

Gannet

Gannets are goose-sized relatives of the boobies (p. 400) that live in temperate regions of the world. The three kinds are considered by some ornithologists to be separate species and by others to be varieties of one species. There is little difference between the three.

Gannets are oceanic birds coming ashore only for the breeding season. They are strong fliers and cover vast distances, especially during the first year of life. Ringing has shown that New Zealand gannets migrate to Australian waters, setting out shortly after they have left the nest and crossing the intervening sea at an average of up to 240 miles a day. The northern gannet migrates south to the Gulf of Mexico and the Canaries.

The gannet of the North Atlantic, known in parts of northern Britain as the solan goose, breeds on both sides of the ocean. In America, there are half a dozen colonies around Newfoundland and the Gulf of St Lawrence. It also breeds off Iceland, the Faeroes and the British Isles, with small colonies in Norway, Brittany and the Channel Islands. The largest colony is on the island of St Kilda. The Cape gannet breeds off South Africa and the Australian or Pacific gannet in the Bass Strait between Australia and Tasmania and North Island, New Zealand.

Gannet pugnacity

Gannets live by feeding on fish and squid, plunging in from a height or diving from the surface. Fish are caught as the birds surface rather than being impaled on the beaks of the gannets as they penetrate the water. The gannets do not dive very deep and will chase their prey, propelling themselves with both feet and wings.

The main food of the northern gannet is haddock, herring, mackerel, saithe, sprat, and whiting. These are important commercially but it is very unlikely that the gannets affect the numbers caught by fishermen. In fact, the commercial catches of herring and other fish around the British Isles are going down, probably because of overfishing, yet the gannet population is steadily rising. So there are almost certainly no direct links between numbers of either the gannets or their prey. The Australian gannet feeds mainly on anchovies although it will take a variety of fish.

Gannet colonies are usually perched on small offshore islands or rocks, often no more than steep-sided towers rearing out of the sea, like Bass Rock on the Firth of Forth or Bird Rock in the Gulf of St Lawrence. The nests are closely packed together, perhaps $2-2\frac{1}{2}$ ft between each, so the cliff ledges and the tops of the rocks or islands are white with birds.

In February, when the rocks are still being

Top: A gannet colony carpets a cliff-top.
Right: Like a diver on a high board, a gannet goes through its take-off procedure.

Eric Hosking

John Barrie

lashed by winter gales, the male gannets appear in the colonies to re-establish ownership of last year's nest or if breeding for the first time they fly low over the colonies looking for abandoned nests. Fights are frequent as gannets defend their nests or seek to oust interlopers. They are not sham fights as often is the case among birds that nest in dense colonies. The gannets grapple each other's bills or grab their opponent's head or neck, shaking, twisting and lunging for up to 2 hours.

chalky white. As the egg is being laid, the gannet bends its tail under its body, directing the egg into the nest. This is probably another adaptation from their original cliff-nesting habit, where it is essential that the egg should not be allowed to roll away. Gannets have no brood patch where the egg is held to keep it warm. Instead the egg is held between the webbed feet. The gannet holds the egg lengthwise under its body and wraps a web around each side of the egg, overlapping underneath. Both parents in-

tors, except on St Kilda and a few other places where man has taken the sitting birds or their young. On Bird Rock, the building of a lighthouse gave access to the gannet colony which was nearly wiped out because the birds were killed for use as fish bait.

The main enemies of the colonies are herring gulls or black-backed gulls that steal eggs. Skuas chase the adults, forcing them to disgorge the food they are carrying back to their chicks.

△ *Open wide: mealtime for a gannet chick.*

Furious fights in courtship
Bryan Nelson, who spent several years studying gannets on Bass Rock, has suggested that gannets originally nested on cliff ledges and the nesting on the flat spaces on top is relatively recent. This would explain several of the gannets' habits. When cliff-nesting birds fight, one of them is sure to be pushed over the edge within a short time, automatically cutting short the fight. Gannets, on the other hand, grapple with their beaks and wrestle to and fro, neither bird appearing to be able to disengage. The fierceness of the gannets' behaviour is continued in their courtship. The females are pecked during mating and whenever the males return to the nests after feeding.

The nests are large, compacted piles of seaweed, grass, earth and all sorts of rubbish including fish nets and tin cans. One list of materials included a gold watch and a set of false teeth. The pile is cemented by droppings and is useful as a jumping-off point for takeoff, as gannets have difficulty taking off from flat ground.

Feet make a hotwater bottle
The single egg, about 3 in. long, is a translucent pale blue at first, later turning to a

cubate, working in shifts of 1–2 days apiece.

Incubation lasts about 44 days. The chick hatches naked but quickly acquires a coat of down. At first it is brooded on top of the parents' feet then later sits by itself in the nest while the parents collect food for it. At Bass Rock the chicks are fed mainly on mackerel which they take by thrusting their heads into the parent's mouth.

When they have fledged at the age of 2 months the young gannets are abandoned by their parents and left to fend for themselves. They leap out of their nests and if they are lucky they immediately become airborne. Otherwise each has to struggle through the colony to the cliff edge, being attacked on the way and perhaps killed by the other gannets. Once airborne, the young gannets can fly quite well, but after they have settled on the sea they cannot rise again. On leaving the nest they are very fat and they spend some time losing weight until they become airborne again and learn to catch their own food.

Violated sanctuary
On their inaccessible stacks and rocks gannets are immune to mammalian preda-

Dive-bombing technique

A flock of gannets feeding is a most spectacular sight. Like boobies, they plunge vertically into the sea, with wings half-closed, from a height of 100 ft or more. There is a continual rain of gannets diving down and disappearing with a spurt of spray. Later they emerge and climb again to rejoin their companions flying around above them before repeating the descent.

Hitting the water at perhaps 100 mph could result in severe injury. But gannets and boobies have very much strengthened skulls that protect the brain. An intricate system of air sacs in the head cushions the impact, and the nostrils open inside the bill so preventing water from entering the air passages.

class	**Aves**
order	**Pelecaniformes**
family	**Sulidae**
genus & species	***Sula bassana*** *common gannet* ***S. capensis*** *cape gannet* ***S. serrator*** *Australian gannet*

Gaper

Normally a bivalve mollusc lives within two shells or valves which can be closed tight or allowed to gape when the animal feeds — but a gaper is a bivalve mollusc which cannot close its shell. The two siphons of a gaper are connected throughout their length and although they may sometimes be withdrawn into the shell they are usually held fully extended. This causes the shell at the hinder end to gape widely. In Britain closely related species of Mya and Lutraria are given the name. Off the coasts of North America there are two species.

The three British species are the sand gaper, or old maid, with a shell nearly 8 in. long, the similar blunt gaper, with a narrower shell, and the small gaper. The sand gaper is also found on the coast of North America. The North American gaper of the Pacific shores from Alaska to San Diego is similar to but slightly smaller than the sand gaper.

Fountains on the shore

Found along the seashore or in shallow water down to 150 ft, the gaper burrows slowly into the mud, using the small foot at its lower end. It normally digs in vertically at 8–12 in. depth, with its long, fringed valve openings at its top end flush with the surface of the mud. A small depression in the mud shows where it lies buried.

When the tide is out, the North American gaper — which rejoices in the alternative names of summer clam, rubber-neck clam, high-neck clam, horse clam, otter-shell clam, and great Washington clam — gives more spectacular evidence of its presence. At fairly regular intervals, its siphons shoot a jet of water to a height of 2–3 ft. These jets are even more powerful when someone walks over the sand. Another water-squirting clam which looks and behaves like a gaper is the geoduck (pronounced go-ee-duck). Both geoduck and gaper are dug out for food, and so — occasionally — are the sand and blunt gapers in Britain.

How the siphon works

These water jets give a good clue to the gaper's methods of feeding and breathing. Water is drawn in through one siphon and passes across the gills, as explained under clam (see clam on page 577). Fine particles of food are extracted and oxygen is taken from the water for breathing. The water is then ejected through the other siphon, carrying with it waste products from the body. The way food is dealt with by the ciliated gills has been described for the cockle (p. 602).

Losing its beard

The sexes are separate, the eggs and milt are shed into the sea through the exhalant siphon. The fertilised egg is developed into the usual veliger larva (see cockle, p 602). When the larva changes into the gaper, it is only ⅟₁₀ in. across, and at first is quite different from the adult. The very small gaper has a relatively large foot and short siphons, and it has a small bunch of byssus threads (see clam, p. 577) for fastening itself to a solid support. Gapers are known to live 17 years.

Food for walruses

Gapers are attacked by different enemies according to where they grow. Everywhere they are eaten by carnivorous sea-snails, such as whelks, which are collectively known as drills, from their habit of drilling holes in the shells with their radulae, or file-like tongues. On the shore, gapers are attacked by seabirds and in some places foxes visit the shore at low-tide and dig out gapers. Fishes with stout jaws for crushing shellfish may take them, and in northern latitudes the blunt gaper forms the main food of the walrus.

Cutting off their feet

Although the double siphon of a gaper is protected by a tough brown skin with two horny valves at the tip, part of it, apparently, is often sacrificed, because these tips are commonly found in the stomachs of halibuts. Nevertheless, these lost portions can be regrown.

Another natural hazard of clams in general is that when violently disturbed they contract the muscles closing their shells so forcibly that a slight blow on the outside will cause their shells to break. A gull seizing one and flying up to 50 ft or so to drop it onto the beach is on to a good thing. The shell will then break as certainly as if dropped onto rock.

Some clams are their own enemies. When suddenly disturbed they may snap their shells so rapidly that they cut off the end of the siphons or the tip of their own foot. Professors GE and Nettie MacGinitie, American marine biologists, report how they found small living animals on the shore which puzzled them. Even with the aid of zoologist colleagues they were unable to classify them. Finally, these 'animals' turned out to be pieces of clam siphon, still capable of muscular contraction and with cilia still beating, hours after they had been cut off by their former owners.

Common otter-shell. When relaxed and undisturbed, the gaper's siphon protrudes from its shell, taking in food and water and discharging body wastes and water. Some gapers are valuable: Mya arenaria, the sand gaper, is well-known to Americans as the soft-shelled clam, and forms the basis of East Coast clam-bakes and chowders.

phylum	**Mollusca**
class	**Bivalvia**
subclass	**Lamellibranchia**
order	**Heterodonta**
family	**Lutraridae**
genus & species	*Lutraria lutraria* common otter-shell
order	**Adapedonta**
family	**Myidae**
genera & species	*Mya arenaria* sand gaper *M. binghami* small gaper *M. truncata* blunt gaper *Schizothaerus nuttallii* N American gaper *others*

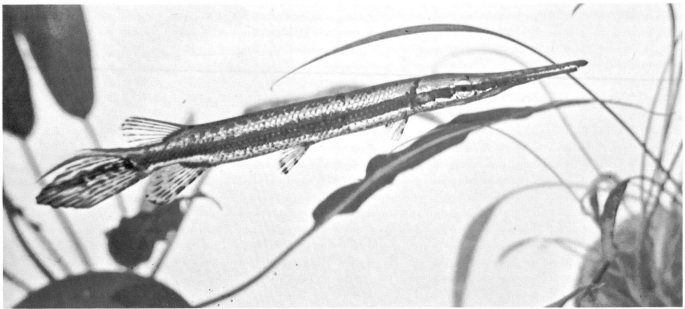

Gene Wolfsheimer

Gar

*These slender pike-like fishes are living
fossils of a family that reached its peak
in the Mesozoic period 70–220 million
years ago. There are seven species living
in the rivers and lakes of North and
Central America.*

*The commonest is the longnose gar, or
billfish, which lives from the Great Lakes
southwards. It is up to 5 ft long, its slim
body covered with a tough armour of
close-set diamond-shaped or rhombic
enamelled (ganoid) scales which do not
overlap in the usual manner of fish scales.
The long snout is a beak; its jaws studded
with small sharp teeth recall those of the
gharial among crocodilians, the beak being
twice as long as the rest of the head.
The dorsal and anal fins are set far back
on the body. The back is olive to silver,
the underside white.*

*The shortnose gar, up to 2 ft long, lives
mainly in the Great Lakes. The tropical
gar of Mexico is said to reach 10 or even
12 ft, and the alligator gar which ranges
from southern United States to Panama
and Cuba is about the same size. Its
snout is very like that of an alligator.*

Indolent fishes

The gars live mainly in still waters, where
they lie almost motionless among water
plants, looking more like floating logs than
fish. They move quietly and slowly to stalk
passing prey, which is seized with a sudden
sideways slash of the snout. Although apparently so lethargic gars can move rapidly
when necessary. Their food is mainly other
fishes but little animal food is refused.
Frogs, salamanders and worms are readily
accepted and the young gar feeds largely on
water insects. They soon take to catching
fish, however, and a young 2 in. gar is on
record as taking 16 young minnows in quick
succession. It is easy to imagine from this
the predatory nature of the gar and why
fishermen hate them, and gars also take

bait from their hooks. A gar can, with one
snap of its jaws, seize a whole group of small
fishes. With larger fish the prey must be
gradually worked round in the mouth into
a position from which it can be swallowed
head first. All food takes 24 hours to digest,
which is slow compared with most other
freshwater fishes.

Eggs and babies stick to rocks

The males mature in 3–4 years, the females
taking 6 years. Spawning is from March to
May in shallow waters, each female being
accompanied by 3 or 4 males. The average
number of eggs laid per female is about
28 000 but may vary from 4 000 to 60 000
according to her size. The eggs are sticky
and cling to rocks and water plants. In a
few days they hatch and the baby fishes fix
themselves to water plants by cement
organs, adhesive discs at the end of the
snout, and hang there until the yolk sac
has been absorbed. After this they swim
freely, feeding at first on mosquito larvae.

Rapid growth

In spite of its reputation for voracity,
justified if by nothing else by its almost
shark-like teeth, a gar has a low food consumption, feeds irregularly and has a slow
rate of digestion. Yet it is one of the fastest
growing of freshwater fishes. In its first
year a young male gar grows on average just
over $\frac{1}{16}$ in. a day to reach $19\frac{1}{2}$ in. by the end
of the first season, the female reaching 22 in.
in the same period. After that growth slows
down to 1 in. a year but continues for 13–14
years in the females, which outlive the males.
Because it moves about so little—even its
feeding is leisurely—and because it has a
high metabolic efficiency (that is, its body
makes the fullest use of all its food), the
energy supplied by the food goes into growing in size instead of being dissipated by
moving about quickly and continuously.

Arrowheads and ploughs

In all probability it is because its scales are
so closely set, forming such a rigid covering,
that a gar must lead an inactive life. This

△ *The dart-shaped body of short-nosed gar
helps it merge with surrounding water plants.*

tough scaly armour of the gar has, however,
proved very useful and been used by
different peoples in different ways. The
original inhabitants of the Caribbean islands
are said to have used the skin, with its
diamond-shaped, closely fitting scales, for
breastplates. Some of the North American
Indians separated the scales and used them
for arrowheads. The early pioneers in what
is now the United States found gar skin
hard enough to cover the blades of their
wooden ploughs.

class	**Osteichthyes**
order	**Amiiformes**
family	**Lepisosteidae**
genus & species	***Lepisosteus osseus*** longnose gar
	L. platystomus shortnose gar
	L. spatula alligator gar
	L. tristoechus tropical gar

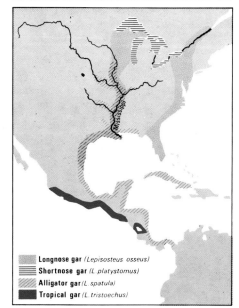

▨ **Longnose gar** *(Lepisosteus osseus)*
▤ **Shortnose gar** *(L. platystomus)*
▨ **Alligator gar** *(L. spatula)*
▮ **Tropical gar** *(L. tristoechus)*

Garden snail

All too familiar to most gardeners, the garden snail is the second largest land snail in Britain. Its shell is up to $1\frac{1}{2}$ in. across, with $4\frac{1}{2}-5$ whorls. Its tabby appearance is due to 5 dark brown spiral bands on a fawn, yellowish or buff background, the bands being broken by streaks of the ground colour making it look mottled. The shell is calcium carbonate (chalk) covered by a glaze of protein material which tends to wear off with age. The snail itself is dark grey. The head has two pairs of tentacles, the larger of which has eyes at the tips and can be pulled inside out by a muscle running up the inside. The smaller pair has other sense organs. When the snail withdraws, the opening into its shell is filled by a collar of soft tissue finely speckled with

Rock-boring snails

Needing calcium for their shells, snails tend to flourish where soils and rocks are rich in it, and they are less fond of clay soils. Where calcium is scarce, the shell may be very thin, as in some populations in the Channel Isles. On the other hand, some areas are notable for the holes bored in limestone by these snails. These are about 1 in. across and may extend 3 or 4 in. upwards into the rock, worn by generations of snails. The garden snail is absent from northern Europe but occurs in the Netherlands, France, Spain, Portugal and around the Mediterranean and the Black Sea. It has also been introduced, or has found its way, to North and South America, Australia, southern Africa, Cuba, Mauritius and St Helena. In Britain it is widespread, except in the north of Scotland, and is most abundant in southern England, especially near the sea, and is found in gardens, hedges and quarries, under cliffs and banks and in old walls, particularly if ivy-covered.

outwards. Evaporation and the production of slime can lead to excessive loss of water but these are greatly reduced when the snail withdraws into its shell, as it does during dry periods. Its rate of living also slows down and months or years can be endured without re-awakening. There are records of snails remaining inactive for as long as 4 years and the Rev W Bingley wrote in 1805 of snails re-awakening after they had been more than 15 years in somebody's collection.

Under normal conditions this sleep may be ended by the return of wet weather, with a dramatic reappearance of active snails. Any deficiency in body water is then made up by absorption through the skin. Consequently, the amount of water in a snail's body is forever fluctuating, and the volume and concentration of the blood varies more particularly.

Home after a meal

Inside the mouth is a hard, curved plate, $2-3$ mm across, called the jaw, and below

Emerging from its shell, a snail spreads its two pairs of horns by turning them inside out, and raises its head to survey the scene before setting off.

Series by Jane Burton: Photo Res.

yellowish grey, and this has a hole, called the pneumostome, passing through it that periodically opens and closes. This lies a little to the animal's right side and leads into the 'lung', a cavity just beneath the shell used in breathing and also, by decreasing in volume, allowing the snail into its shell.

The garden snail **Helix aspersa** (aspersa for 'besprinkled') is often known as the common snail and 'garden snail' is commonly applied to **Cepaea hortensis,** a close relative of the banded snail (p. 134). Confusion is avoided if one uses the proper scientific name.

Freak shells are sometimes found in which the whorls twist in the reverse direction or are separated, making a corkscrew or cornucopia. Sometimes the colouring may be a more or less uniform yellow. Artificial monstrosities were once made for amusement. A snail would be removed carefully and placed in a shell of similar size but of another species. Eventually the snail would anchor itself in the shell and lay down new shell whorls of a different pattern and colour.

Multi-purpose slimes

A snail moves by waves of muscular activity passing forwards along the sole of the foot. Generally 7 at a time can be seen as it moves over a sheet of glass. It gives out slime from just behind the head to make its slime track. This is not a continuous smear, but a series of patches where the foot has touched the ground. Slime of other kinds is given out from other parts of the body, including a bright yellow slime discharged when the snail is irritated. Slime, secreted by the collar, dries to form one or a series of membranes, sealing the opening of the shell when the snail is withdrawn, or it may be used to seal the opening against a flat surface.

Snails spend much of their lives drawn inside the shell during dry spells and in winter. Preparation for hibernation may begin as early as September, the snails congregating among the roots of shrubs or in old walls or burying themselves several inches in the earth, the mouth of the shell then being sealed. Young snails may spend a shorter time hibernating or may awaken temporarily on mild days in winter, but adults seldom stir until the following April.

The moist surface of a snail, unlike our own skin, allows water to pass inwards or

this is the file-like radula or tongue with 15 000 file-like horny teeth arranged in rows (see abalone p. 12).

Garden snails, generally less of a pest in gardens than slugs, eat the leaves of many plants including lettuce, hops, primrose, nasturtium, alder and, more remarkably, nettle and holly. They are fond of fruit and they may eat dead slugs and earthworms. Spindle and yew are said to be poisonous to them, and one may sometimes find large numbers of empty shells under yew trees. Snails will also eat paper. They have a well-developed homing instinct and regularly return from their foraging expeditions to the same roosting place, which is often communal. Gardeners who try to get rid of snails by throwing them over a fence should know they will return, even climbing the fence to do so.

Uneven life history

Each snail has both male and female organs, being hermaphrodite. Mating, which may last half a day, takes place throughout spring and summer. Two snails, after mutual fondling, plunge their 'love darts' into each other. These 'love darts' are small chalky spicules only $\frac{1}{3}$in long, slightly curved and with four longitudinal blades, ejected

999

James Carr

from special muscular sacs. Then follows an exchange of sperm contained in long packets called spermatophores. The eggs, 40–100 or so, are laid soon after in holes in the soil and covered over. They are slightly oval, $\frac{1}{6}$ in. long, with tough, whitish coverings. They hatch in 2–4 weeks.

Although eggs are laid soon after pairing, the sperm can survive for a long while after being exchanged so eggs can be laid months later without further mating. In another species this interval has been known to extend as long as 4 years.

The young snails hatch with a glossy, unbanded shell of about $1\frac{1}{2}$ whorls and grow to a third or half of the final size by the time they are ready to hibernate. Growth, like their lives so influenced by the weather, is not even. It involves the periodic rapid addition of shell around the aperture, sometimes as much as 1 in. in 2 weeks. The outer protein layer is produced first. Individuals have been known to live 5–10 years, but 2 years is more usual.

A neglected delicacy

Enemies are rats, moles, hedgehogs, field voles, rabbits, ducks, geese, domestic fowls, thrushes, blackbirds, glowworms, certain beetles and flies—and man. In Britain winkles (sea snails) and oysters are eaten with relish, and sometimes the Roman or edible snail. But although land snails of various kinds are eaten on the European Continent, few people in Britain can be persuaded to eat the garden snail. This was not always so, and in the 19th century 'wall fish', as garden snails were called, were on sale in markets at Bath, Bristol, Swindon, Covent Garden in London, and probably elsewhere. The glassmen of Newcastle enjoyed a feast of them once a year until at least 1880. An excellent imitation cream could be made from milk plus the slime.

PA Bowman

Above and top: Garden snails mating. Although snails are hermaphrodite, they reproduce by exchanging the products of their gonads after stabbing each other with their 'love darts'.

Shells found in Wick Barrow, Stogursey, suggest that garden snails were eaten in the early Bronze Age, about 1 800 BC, and they seem to have been used in Roman-British times in the west of England. The Romans cultivated snails in 'cochlearia', the first of which were set up about 50 BC by Fulvius Hirpinus at Tarquinium. This was recorded by Pliny the Elder who also recommended snails (but not *aspersa*) for coughs and stomach aches (to be taken in odd numbers!). Snails and slugs have been used to treat a variety of ailments, notably pulmonary tuberculosis, coughs and colds. In Yorkshire, at one time, they provided a greenish salve for corns, and in the 1880s, plasters, sold at a penny each in London,

WM Scott

Snails lay clusters of whitish eggs in the soil soon after mating. These take 2–4 weeks to hatch, and the baby snails emerge complete with a glossy, unbanded shell.

were made from papers over which garden snails had crawled.

Two additional uses for the garden snail were recorded by Martin Lister in 1678. He noted that the fluid obtained by pricking snails was used in bleaching wax for artistic purposes and also for making a firm cement when mixed with the white of egg.

phylum	**Mollusca**
class	**Gastropoda**
order	**Pulmonata**
family	**Helicidae**
genus & species	***Helix aspersa***

Garter snake

Garter snakes are the commonest and most familiar snakes of the United States and Canada. They also occur in Mexico. They are found farther north than any other reptile in the Western Hemisphere, the common garter snake as far north as 67 degrees latitude, in the Yukon. Garter snakes are non-venomous, slender, marked with longitudinal stripes, commonly 2 ft, sometimes 3 ft long, the record being 5 ft. The common garter snake may be black, brown or olive with three yellowish, orange or red stripes. The stripes may be vivid or dull. The belly is usually yellow or greenish. All-black individuals may occur. One species, known as the ribbon snake, has three golden-yellow stripes, and its scales are more markedly keeled than in other garter snakes. It lives in southeastern Canada and the United States east of the Mississippi, especially in marshy areas, and takes readily to water. Another subspecies, the western ribbon snake **Thamnophis sauritus proximus***, lives west of the Mississippi.*

From sea level to the Rockies
Garter snakes live in a variety of habitats from sea level to high up in the Rockies. The mountain garter snake is the only reptile in the Rocky Mountain National Park. The Mexican garter snake is found up to 13 000 ft. They are, however, often restricted to the neighbourhood of streams and lakes in the western half of the United States but are found almost everywhere in the humid eastern half. The plains garter snake is found even in the suburbs of towns such as New York and Chicago, where they hibernate in cracks in the ground near the bases of buildings.

They are the last reptiles to go into winter quarters and the first to come out, as early as March, from a hibernaculum which may be as deep as 3 ft underground. A saying of one tribe of North American Indians is that the first clap of thunder brings them out of hibernation.

It is said there is one or another subspecies of garter snake in every state, and in places the species overlap. Where they do there is no competition. The different species tend to occupy slightly different habitats, one preferring damper ground than the other, for example, and usually they show slightly different food preferences. They also tend to breed at different times.

Early food is worms
Young garter snakes feed almost entirely on earthworms in their first year. After that, although worms are the chief item in their diet, they also eat frogs, toads and salamanders, sometimes fish and occasionally birds' eggs. Large garter snakes may eat mice.

Very large litters
Mating takes place near the winter quarters, soon after the snakes come out in late winter. The male has tiny barbels on his chin which

he passes along the female's back as he prepares to mate with her. Once mating is over the snakes disperse to their summer ranges. The young are born alive in summer in litters of usually 50−60 but the number may vary from 12 to 78. The newly-born garter snake is 6 in. long. It grows a foot a year for the first 2−3 years, is mature at 2 years old, is ready to mate in its third spring and may live 12 years. There is, however, a very heavy death-rate during the first few months, due mainly to predators and deaths from starvation.

Killed in error

Their enemies are snake-eating snakes, hawks, owls, skunks and domestic cats. All-black individuals, or those with indistinct stripes, are apt to be killed by people in mistake for poisonous snakes. They are also killed in large numbers on the roads.

Garter snakes take readily to water; this wandering garter has hunted down a small speckled dace and is dragging it onto a stretch of floating algae before tucking in.

A garter snake's defence is to give out an obnoxious fluid from a pore on either side of the vent. It may bite but this has little effect on the human skin.

Some snakes lay eggs; others, such as garter snakes, bear their young alive. The first is called ovipary, the second is ovovivipary and in this the eggs remain inside the mother until they hatch. In both the eggs contain yolk for feeding the developing embryo but in ovoviviparous snakes oxygen for breathing and moisture must be supplied by the maternal tissues, so the shells must be very thin, virtually no more than a transparent membrane in most cases. In garter snakes, as well as European adders, sea snakes and the Australian

copperheads, a sort of placenta is formed to carry nourishment from mother to developing young. It is a very simple affair, nothing like as efficient as the placenta of mammals, but it is enough to supplement the yolk supply already in the egg.

The main advantages of ovovivipary are that there is no chance of the eggs drying up and the temperature remains fairly constant. The mother can choose basking areas with suitable temperatures. This is important in latitudes where summers are short and where even summer temperatures are not high. Add to this the advantages of having even a simple placenta and it is easy to see why garter snakes can live so far north. The disadvantages of ovovivipary are that the mother is encumbered, less agile and therefore handicapped in hunting and in dodging enemies. In most species this is minimized by the broods

△ *Colourful version of the common garter, with three stripes of vivid yellow.*

carried being small in numbers. It is the more remarkable, therefore, that garter snakes should commonly have 50–60, even 78 young in a brood.

class	**Reptilia**
order	**Squamata**
suborder	**Serpentes**
family	**Colubridae**
genus & species	***Thamnophis sirtalis*** common garter snake ***T. elegans*** mountain garter snake ***T. elegans vagrans*** *wandering garter snake* ***T. radix*** *plains garter snake* ***T. sauritus*** *ribbon snake, others*

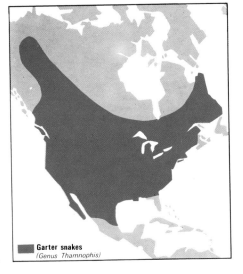

Garter snakes
(Genus Thamnophis)

Gaur

The gaur is the largest species of wild cattle, usually standing $5\frac{1}{2}-6$ ft, but one male shot in Burma stood 7 ft high with a girth of $8\frac{1}{2}$ ft. The average weight of males is just under 1 ton with females somewhat smaller. Both sexes are black, with legs whitish from the knees and hocks down. Young gaurs are brownish-orange until they reach maturity. The horns are semicircular, curving sideways and corrugated at the base. They grow to 25 in. Male gaurs are immensely muscular and usually have a dewlap.

Closely related to the gaur are the banteng and the kouprey. Both are smaller than the gaur. Gaurs are still common in many places and banteng are not rare, but the kouprey is scarce. The male bantengs are black in the southern parts of their range and tawny in the north. Females are khaki or tawny. The legs and rump are white. The kouprey is the same size as the banteng. Both sexes are grey, with white patches on shoulders and rump as well as the legs.

The gaur lives in India, Burma, Vietnam and Malaya, where it is called the seladang. Recently it has been found in Yunnan, in southern China. The banteng inhabits Burma and Vietnam, is not found in Malaya or Sumatra, but is found again in Java and Borneo. The kouprey is restricted to northern Cambodia and southern Laos.

Cows lead the herds

These huge wild cattle live in mountain forests in small herds that are basically associations of cows with their calves. In January and February a herd of gaur usually consists of 5 or 6 animals of which 1 or 2 will be bulls. Then, in April or May, bulls join the herds for the rut, swelling the numbers to 9 or 10, although individual bulls may move from herd to herd. In May or June, they leave to form small herds of bulls only, or to live singly.

Each herd has a home range in which it is usually to be found. The home range is not exclusive, and several herds may cover one area, wandering 2–5 miles in a day. Sometimes the small herds join together so 50 or more gaur may be seen feeding in one valley. While they are feeding, one member of the herd, usually a cow, may stand, with head raised, on a mound or anthill, presumably acting as a sentinel, giving a loud whistling snort if danger threatens. A cow will also lead the herd while it is on the move.

Both gaur and banteng have been domesticated. The domestic gaur, called the gayal or mithan, is sometimes said to be a separate species, formed by the crossing of wild gaur and common cattle. The gayal has shorter horns and a wider forehead than the gaur. It is kept only by the Nagas

▷*Heavyweights in the wild: Indian gaur cattle in a forest clearing.*

and Mishmis of Assam who use it as a status symbol and for sacrifices, rather than for meat or milk. Banteng are domesticated on the islands of Java and Bali where they are the common domestic stock.

Fond of salt licks

Gaurs feed mainly on grass or occasionally bamboo shoots, but also eat leaves and nuts. They feed in the open, usually at night, returning to the forest to chew the cud during the day. Like many jungle animals, gaurs are very fond of visiting salt licks. These are specially provided by man as a lure when gaurs are needed for domestication.

Wild bull rings

During the rut the bulls move from herd to herd, each mating with many cows, and because the herd is continually changing the hierarchy of bulls is continually changing. The dominant bulls are the largest and they display at each other by standing broadside with head lowered, 10–20 ft from their rival. Then one begins to circle while the other stands still, except to remain broadside-on. This display may last 10–15 minutes, or even as much as an hour, until one bull is intimidated and moves away.

There is no strict breeding season but the peak of the rut is in March and April when the bulls have joined the cows. Gesta-tion takes 9 months, so most calves are born in December or January. The cows leave the herd to give birth, returning after about 4 days.

Mass attack

Tigers may kill gaur calves, but are no match for an adult. A bull gaur advances with head lowered and sweeping up and down, threatening to impale any potential enemy on its horns. Sometimes the whole herd will advance *en masse*, presenting a formid-able array of horns.

The last great beast

In 1937, the director of Vincennes Zoo was travelling through Cambodia, when he came across the head of an odd-looking ox hang-ing as a trophy in the house of a vet, Mon-sieur Sauvel. Thus the kouprey was first made known to western science and became the last large mammal to be found. It had probably been overlooked because it is rare and lives in country that is hardly pene-trated by westerners. When it was first seen it was probably mistaken for banteng or for domestic cattle that had gone wild. Even now little is known about it. It has been suggested that koupreys are cross-breeds between banteng and gaur, Indian buffalo or zebu, the Oriental domestic cattle. An-other suggestion is that they are the

△ *A family of banteng, probably a smaller domesticated variety of the gaur.*

descendants of the domestic stock of the ancient Khmer empire. Both its form and its behaviour, however, suggest that the kouprey is a true species. The shape of the horns differs from those of other cattle in Asia, being cylindrical in section, recurved in males and lyre-shaped in females. Old male kouprey fray their horns near the tips, apparently by rubbing them on tree-trunks or anthills. Fraying has not been recorded in other wild cattle, except the European bison.

It is very likely that the kouprey forms a link between the gaur and banteng on the one hand and domestic cattle and the aurochs, the now-extinct wild ancestor of European cattle, on the other (see p. 530). As such it is of interest to scientists, but the population, estimated at 500-1 000 in 1952, is probably nearly extinct because of the recent wars in its homeland.

class	**Mammalia**
order	**Artiodactyla**
family	**Bovidae**
genus & species	***Bos gaurus*** *gaur* ***B. banteng*** *banteng* ***B. sauveli*** *kouprey*

Sally Anne Thompson

Gazelle

Gazelles are slender antelopes, dainty and graceful in movement. The males have sweeping, lyre-shaped horns but the females have short spikes or no horns at all. There are 10 species of true gazelle, genus **Gazella**, in Asia and northern and eastern Africa. The best known are, the smallest of all, the Dorcas gazelle, of Algeria to Egypt and the Sudan, only 21 in. at the shoulder, and Grant's and Thomson's gazelles of East Africa. There used to be vast herds of the last two before they were slaughtered by hunters or driven from their homes by the spread of agriculture. All are fawn-coloured with a white rump and belly, and a dark band along the flanks. They have a white streak on either side of the face from eye to muzzle and usually a dark streak below this. Grant's gazelle, together with Soemmerring's and the red-necked gazelles, are the largest, 33−37 in. at the shoulder with a white wedge-shaped patch on the rump.

Three other species are also known as gazelles. These are the Tibetan, Prze-walski's and the Mongolian gazelle, all of the genus **Procapra**. They live on the grassy plains of Siberia, Mongolia, China and Tibet. They lack the glands on face and 'knees' that are features of the true gazelles.

Common or rare

Gazelles usually live in dry country, although some live on fertile plains. Most species are widespread and exist in large numbers. Speke's gazelle, with an inflatable swelling on its nose, is found only in the deserts of Somalia; and Loder's gazelle, a very pale species with narrow, spreading hooves, is restricted to the Ergs, the dune areas of the Sahara. The red gazelle is known from only four specimens, all bought at souks, or markets, in Algeria.

The goitred gazelle, named for the small cartilaginous swelling in the throats of the males, is also a desert animal, living from Arabia to Mongolia. Like many other desert animals it migrates in search of food. In Soviet Asia, around Lake Balkash, the herds come down from the mountains to escape from winter snows and in Kazakhstan they migrate south some 300 miles across the steppes in winter. In the summer they return to feed on fresh vegetation growing under the snow. During the summer a herd may range over a few square miles but in winter it may have to move over 100 square miles in search of food.

△ A couple of Thomson's gazelle, enjoying a quiet scratch on the high veld.

Water from absorbent shrubs

Gazelles eat grass when it is available, but in dry country they browse low-growing bushes and succulents. Many of them can go without drinking for long periods. Some Grant's gazelle were watched during a drought in East Africa when they ate mainly a certain dry shrub. Experiments showed that at night, when the relative humidity of the atmosphere was higher, this shrub absorbed water from the air, and so by eating at night the gazelles were able to get all the water they needed.

Territorial bucks

The goitred gazelle has a fixed breeding season. In September the bucks join the herds of does and begin to separate them into groups of 2−5, each protected by one buck. At the end of the rut in December the doe herds reassemble. Other species in more tropical areas have no fixed breeding season. In East Africa the strongest bucks of Thomson's gazelle establish territories of 20−60 ft diameter in open country which they defend against other bucks. When the herd, mainly of does, passes through the territory, the buck mounts several does. Any bucks travelling with the does are tolerated, but the rest form a separate herd

on the edges of the open country. In the dry season, the bucks leave their territories and join the main herd migrating to fresh pastures. When they return the territories have to be set up again, and it may not be the same animals that are successful in doing so.

When first born the young crouch hidden until they are strong enough to run. In a few days they can run fast enough to keep up with their mothers.

Wary but unafraid

In East Africa Thomson's gazelles are preyed upon by all four large predators: lions, cheetahs, leopards and cape hunting dogs, as well as hyaenas. Eagles also take the young. In Asia, wolves and tigers prey on gazelles. It is the bucks of the all male herds that suffer most. They live on the fringes of the bush where their enemies can lie in wait.

Although built for running, gazelles do not use their speed to the full. They will run for 200–300 yd, then stop and look back at their enemies, or else they will run about, jinking, rather than trying to put as much space between themselves and their enemies as possible. By contrast, they approach waterholes very carefully. The main herd halts some 200 yd from the water, then a few young bucks will rush up to the water's edge, quickly look round, then dash back to the herd. This is repeated two or three times, before the herd, convinced that there is no danger, comes down to drink.

Domesticated dorcas

Gazelles could be one of the greatest sources of animal protein in the dry parts of Africa and Asia, even though their numbers have been reduced by overhunting. In Kazakhastan, in Asia, for example, where they have been hard hit, there are 100 000 gazelles still alive. The domestication of gazelles along the lines being carried out with eland (p. 835) would be no new undertaking. The dorcas gazelle was apparently domesticated by the Ancient Egyptians and the Romans. About 7 000 BC gazelle meat formed an important item in the diet of the people of Jericho, and in Egypt writings in a tomb dated 2 500 BC indicate that the occupant had owned 1 135 head of gazelle. Later gazelles were kept by the Romans. Paintings in Pompeii show them in butchers' shops and they were also used for drawing children's chariots. Their skins were used for leather, their horns for knife handles and their ankle bones for dice.

Gazelle portraits
Gazelle species differ only slightly, and one distinguishing feature is seen in the males — the difference between their sweeping lyre-shaped horns. The females usually have stumpy spikes or no horns at all.
1. Grant's gazelle.   2. Mongolian gazelle.
3. Thomson's gazelle.   4. Goitred gazelle.
5. Dorcas gazelle.
Left: Siesta time — a male Grant's gazelle lies lazily in the afternoon heat near a female, while a herd of zebra grazes peacefully close by.

class	**Mammalia**
order	**Artiodactyla**
family	**Bovidae**
genera & species	*Gazella cuvieri* Thomson's gazelle
	G. dorcas dorcas gazelle
	G. granti Grant's gazelle
	G. subgutturosa goitred gazelle
	Procapra gutturosa Mongolian gazelle

Anthony Maynard

Jane Burton: Photo Res

Gecko

Geckos form a family of lizards noted for the large number of species, the structure of their feet, their voices, the differences in the shape of their tails, and for the ease with which some of them will live in houses. The smallest is $1\frac{1}{3}$ in. long; the largest—the tokay—may be 14 in. long.

Geckos are found in all warm countries: 41 species in Africa, 50 in Madagascar, about 50 in Australia, the same in the West Indies, with others in southern and southeast Asia, Indonesia, the Pacific islands and New Zealand, and South America. There are geckos in the desert

regions of Mexico and southern California. Several have been introduced into Florida from the Caribbean islands. Spain and Dalmatia, in southern Europe, have the same wall gecko as North Africa.

A liking for houses

The majority of geckos live in trees, some live among rocks, others live on the sandy ground of deserts. Tree geckos find in human habitations conditions similar to, or better than, those of their natural habitat: natural crevices in which to rest or take refuge and plenty of insects, especially at night when insects are attracted to lights. Because geckos can cling to walls or hang upside-down from ceilings they can take full

△ Pinhole sight: pupils shrunk to four tiny holes, to keep out excessive glare of the sun.

advantage of these common insect resting places, and so many of them are now known as house geckos.

Hooked to the ceiling

Most geckos can cling to smooth surfaces. Their toes may be broad or expanded at the tips with flaps of skin (lamellae) arranged transversely or fanwise. The undersides of the toes look like suction pads but apparently no suction is involved, nor are the undersides sticky. They have numerous microscopic hooks that catch in the slightest irregularities, even those in the surface of glass, and so a gecko can cling to all but the most highly polished surfaces. The hooks are directed backwards and downwards and to disengage them the toe must be lifted upwards from the tip. As a result, a gecko running up a tree or a wall or along a ceiling must curl and uncurl its toes at each step with a speed faster than the eye can follow. Some of the hooks are so small the high power of a microscope is needed to see them, yet a single toe armed with numbers of these incredibly small hooks can support several times the weight of a gecko's body. In addition to the hooks, most species have the usual claw at the tip of the toe which also can be used in clinging. One species has microscopic hooks on the tip of the tail and these help in clinging.

Tails for all tastes

The tail is long and tapering, rounded or slightly flattened and fringed with scales, according to the species, or it may be flattened and leaf-like. A South American gecko has a swollen turnip-shaped tail. It has been named *Thecadactylus rapicaudus* (*rapi* for turnip, *caudus* for tail). The flying gecko of southeast Asia has a leaf-like tail, a wide flap of skin along each flank, a narrow flap along each side of the head and flaps along the hind margins of the limbs. Should the gecko fall it spreads its limbs, the flaps spread and the reptile parachutes safely down.

Geckos can throw off their tails, like the more familiar lizards, and grow new ones. In some species 40% have re-grown tails. Sometimes the tail is incompletely thrown and hangs by a strip of skin. As a new tail grows the old one heals and a 2-tailed gecko results. Even 3-tailed geckos have been seen. Temperature is important in growing a new tail. It has been found that when the wall gecko of southern Europe and North Africa grows a new tail with the air temperature at 28°C/82°F it is short and covered with large overlapping scales. With the temperature around 35°C/95°F the new tail is long and is covered with small scales.

Permanent pair of spectacles

One difference between snakes and lizards is that the former have no eyelids. In most geckos the eyelids are permanently joined and there is a transparent window in the lower lid. The few geckos that are active by day have rounded pupils to the eyes. The rest are active by night and have vertical slit-pupils like cats. In some species the sides of the pupils are lobed or notched in four places, and when the pupils contract they leave four apertures, the size of pinholes each one of which will focus the image onto the retina.

Surprisingly small clutches

All geckos except for a few species in New Zealand, which bear live young, lay eggs

Top: Close pursuit. As firm as the flies it is hunting, a diurnal gecko **Phelsuma vinsoni** *pauses on a vertical tree-trunk, unaware of the apparent impossibility of its position.*
Right: Living crampons. Geckos get a grip from tiny hooks in the flaps of skin on their feet.
Far right: After partial loss, regrowth and healing, the result is a three-tailed gecko.

Anthony Banister: NHPA

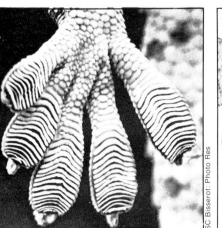

SC Bisserot: Photo Res

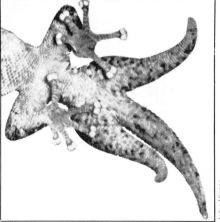

John Visser

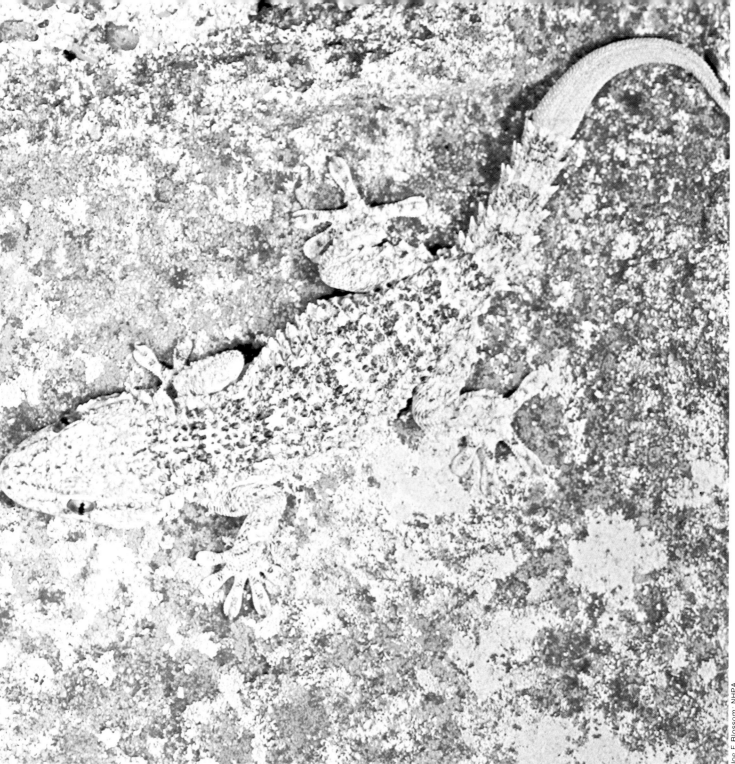

with a tough white shell. Usually there are two in a clutch, sometimes only one. The eggs are laid under bark or under stones and take several months to hatch.

The ghostly gecko

Geckos eat only insects. They are harmless and wholly beneficial to man, yet among the people of Africa, South America, Malaysia and the aboriginals of Australia there are widespread beliefs that their bite makes them dangerous to handle. Possibly such beliefs spring from some of the more remarkable species, like the gecko that stalks insects as a cat does a mouse, even lashing its tail from side to side just before the final pounce. Then there are the web-footed

geckos living on the sand dunes of Southwest Africa. They not only use the webbed feet to run over loose sand but also to burrow. They scrape the sand away with the forefoot of one side and shovel it back with the hind-foot of the same side while balancing on the feet of the other side. Then they change over. They walk with the body raised high and the tail held up and arched.

One web-footed gecko has a delicate beauty. It is pinkish-brown with a lemon yellow stripe along its flank. Its eye has brilliant yellow lids, the iris is black, patterned with gold and coppery tints, while the edges of the vertical pupil are chalky white. Its skin is so transparent its spine and some of its internal organs can be seen clearly. GK Brain, writing in *African Wild*

Not good enough: regrown tail of **Tarantola manritanica** *shows that, despite camouflage, only desperate measures saved its life.*

Life, claims its two ear openings are almost in direct connection, so by looking into one earhole the light coming in through the other can be seen.

class	**Reptilia**
order	**Squamata**
suborder	**Sauria**
family	**Gekkonidae**
genus & species	*Gekko gecko others*

Genet

The genet looks like a cross between a tabby cat and a mongoose. **With the civets and mongooses, genets make up the family Viverridae that lies between the weasel family (Mustelidae) and the cat family (Felidae). Three genets are well known and numerous; three are rare and little known.**

The feline or small spotted genet is cat-like but more slender, elegant in build and graceful in movement. Up to 40 in. total length, of which nearly half is tail, its fur is soft and spotted with brown to black on a light ground colour. The head tapers to a pointed muzzle; the ears are large and the whiskers long. The tail is ringed with dark and light bands, and there is a crest of long black hairs along the back which is raised in moments of excitement. The legs are short, the paws are small and the toes have retractile claws.

The feline genet ranges over most of Africa apart from desert and semi-desert, and is also found in Spain and southern France, but the blotched or tigrine genet is more numerous throughout Africa. It is similar to the feline genet in form and habits but it has larger spots on a more yellowish ground and no crest along the back. The rusty-spotted genet is like the blotched genet except for its more reddish spots and it is found south of Tanzania. Some scientists believe it to be a colour variety of the blotched genet. The Abyssinian genet of the highlands of Ethiopia is small, has ash-coloured fur with longitudinal black stripes and is very rarely seen. The Victorian genet is like the feline genet but has richer markings. It lives in the Ituri Forest in Zaire and is known almost entirely from skins brought back by pygmy hunters of the Ituri. The first skin sent to London by Sir Harry Johnston in 1911 was obtained in the region of Lake Victoria, but the animal does not live there.

The water genet is known from only three skins. It is the size of a domestic cat, has a rich chestnut fur with white markings on the face and a black bushy tail. It was unknown, except to the local people, until 1919.

Ghostly markings have a purpose

A notable feature of genets is their white face markings. They bring to mind the white facial markings on badgers and foxes, two other nocturnal animals, and the markings of the genet may provide a clue to the use of these. When a genet is seen on a dark night, these white marks on the face stand out in the same way as the luminous paint on a clock face. To only a slightly lesser extent the pale whitish parts of the pattern

▷ *The genet: quick as a cat, curious as a mongoose, it even looks like a cross between them.*

on its body and tail also stand out in the dark. The best comparison is with the way the lights of a ship stand out on a dark night, so although the rest of it is obscured by blackness we still know it is a ship. So we can imagine a genet can recognise another genet in the dark by the ghostly white pattern of its body and tail, or, when seen head-on, by the white markings on the face.

Sure-footed night climber

The feline genet lives alone (at most in pairs) in bush country, sleeping by day among the branches and hunting by night. It can move swiftly over the ground, with the body held low and tail straight out behind, in an almost snake-like movement. It is most at home in bushes and trees, a skilful sure-footed climber, stalking its prey like a cat and seizing it with a swift sharp pounce. Normally it is silent but when alarmed or about to attack it purrs loudly with the sound of a kettle boiling, raising the crest on its back and fluffing the hair of its tail to form a 'bottle-brush'—typical mongoose behaviour when danger is imminent.

Genets are typical carnivores and their canine teeth, though small, are needle-sharp. They feed on any small animal food, especially small rodents, birds and insects, particularly night-flying moths and beetles. A small amount of grass is eaten fairly regularly.

Hidden secrets of breeding

Little is known of the breeding. In the northern parts of its range the genet appears to have 2—3 in a litter, born in spring after a gestation of 10—11 weeks. The nest is in a hollow in a tree or among rocks. In South Africa, at least, there is a second litter in autumn.

Animal night-craft

We, who move about by day or carry a lamp at night, may wonder how an animal that hunts at night among branches can find its way so surely when moving at speed. Perhaps the behaviour of a tame genet tells us this. When first put into a strange room, with branches for it to climb over, the genet will make a circuit of the room, going over

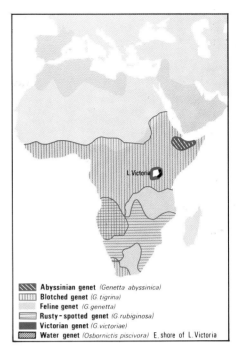

▨	**Abyssinian genet** (Genetta abyssinica)
⦀	**Blotched genet** (G. tigrina)
░	**Feline genet** (G.genetta)
▦	**Rusty-spotted genet** (G.rubiginosa)
▪	**Victorian genet** (G victoriae)
▧	**Water genet** (Osbornictis piscivora) E. shore of L.Victoria

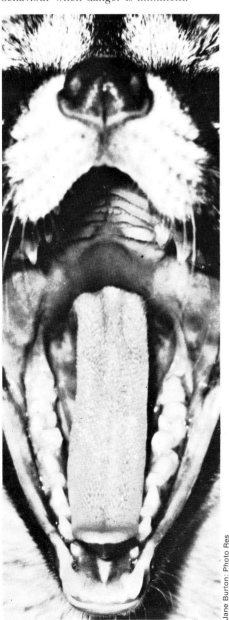

Far left: After a stealthy stalk and quick pounce, a feline genet settles down to a meal.
Left: Prey's-eye view: a genet yawn shows typical carnivore teeth, relatively small, perhaps, but needle-sharp.
Above: Inquisitive, if a little wary, a pair of genet kittens explore the world around them.

the floor and over every branch and other solid object. It goes very slowly, putting each foot down in turn and not putting its weight on that foot until it is sure of its foothold. At the same time it is investigating everything around, with its nose, probably also with its eyes; and since its ears are quivering all the time it is probably bringing the sense of hearing to bear as well.

Having thoroughly investigated the whole of its surroundings in this tediously slow and painstaking way, it repeats the circuit, this time going slightly faster. At the completion of this second circuit it makes a third, this time rapidly. From then on it can race around in total darkness and never put a foot wrong. So far as we can see it

memorizes the whole of its surroundings mainly by touch and smell, perhaps by sight and hearing to a lesser extent.

One genet, put into a fresh cage furnished with branches, slipped at one spot in its first circuit so that it swung under the branch and had to do a 'handspring' to regain its position on the branch. It lived many years in this same cage and always, whenever it came to this same spot on the branch, it swung under it and did a handspring, just as it had on the first occasion.

class	**Mammalia**
order	**Carnivora**
family	**Viverridae**
genera & species	***Genetta abyssinica*** *Abyssinian genet*
	G. genetta *feline genet*
	G. rubiginosa *rusty-spotted genet*
	G. tigrina *blotched genet*
	G. victoriae *Victorian genet*
	Osbornictis piscivora *water genet*

Gerbil

Gerbils, or sand rats, live in desert or semi-desert parts of Africa and Asia. There are many species going by different names — usually describing their characters — such as naked-soled gerbils, fat-tailed mice, and fat sand rats. Two genera are known as jirds, while another whose habits have not yet been recorded is called the ammodille. Gerbils are rat-like and belong to the same family as the common rat, but in some features of appearance and habits they resemble the jerboas or desert rats. The fur is fawn on the upper parts, the hairs often tipped with black making it darker. The under-parts are white. In most species the tail is long and slender often with a small tuft of hairs at the tip, but the fat-tailed gerbil has a very short plump tail. The hindlegs are long, and with the long tail give the gerbils a kangaroo-like appearance.

Most gerbils are found in Africa, especially around the Sahara, but the large naked-soled gerbils live as far south as South Africa, spreading over most of the continent except the equatorial forests. These gerbils, also known as Indian gerbils, are also found in Asia from Turkey and Arabia to India and Sri Lanka. Others are found in Asia; great gerbils and Przewalski's gerbils are limited to the central Asian deserts of Mongolia, Turkestan and Iran.

Desert hopper

Although they are sometimes found in bush or scrub country, the typical home of gerbils is in the dry, sparsely covered regions around deserts. They have many of the features found in desert animals: the bullae or earbones are large, indicating sensitive hearing and water is conserved so some gerbils can live almost indefinitely without drinking. They live in burrows and are usually nocturnal, so avoiding the worst of the sun's heat. Some species have hairy soles on their hindfeet which probably insulate them from the hot sand and many travel by leaping when in a hurry. This is a common feature of desert rodents, such as the jerboa or the kangaroo rat of North American deserts, and is thought to be an economical method of moving about in search of the scant supplies of food in dry regions. The Indian gerbil has been given the name of antelope rat for it progresses in bounds of 15–16 ft.

The habits of gerbils are not well known as most are nocturnal, but many are now kept in laboratories as experimental animals and they are becoming popular as pets. They are expert burrowers and need to be kept in a cage with plenty of earth or sand. Some species make only a simple short burrow. The entrance may be blocked with loose earth, presumably to keep out either enemies or the heat. Other gerbils make complicated systems of burrows with several entrances, and chambers where they make their nests or store food. Often several gerbils make their tunnels close to each other, forming distinct colonies. Observations of great gerbils in winter showed that they never strayed far from their burrows. Footprints in the snow were never found more than 60 ft from a burrow's entrance and most trails never went this far. These gerbils became less active when temperatures fell and the snow became deeper. By midwinter only a few entrances remained open.

Food stored in burrows

Gerbils live mainly on the herbs that flourish in desert country during winter and spring. Leaves, seeds, flowers and roots of many different kinds of plants are eaten, and are often stored in the burrow for future use. The great gerbil stores winter supplies either in the burrow or just outside where they can easily be dug out of the snow. Over 100 lb of food has been found in one burrow. A few gerbils are also carnivorous. The short-eared gerbils sometimes feed on locusts and grasshoppers which they take back to the burrows and eat at the entrance, scattering the discarded wings and bodies. The Indian gerbil occasionally eats the young of its own kind and takes eggs and chicks from nests of birds.

Foot-stamping drummers

Some gerbils have breeding seasons restricted to a few months in the year, while others breed all the year round. The breeding habits of most species are unknown. Both sexes of the great gerbil mark their territories by rubbing their bellies on rocks, which transfers a musky secretion from glands on their bellies. A common habit of gerbils is to stamp their hindfeet, presumably to advertise themselves. It is possible to hear the slow, muffled thud coming from the burrows. The males will also fight, sitting back like kangaroos on their hindfeet while they bite and kick.

There may be several litters a year of 1–8 babies. The birth takes place after about 3 weeks gestation and the young stay below ground for about another 3 weeks. Then

◁ Apprehension: A gerbil swings on to its hindlegs to look round before bounding away.
▷ Mid-leap: **Gerbillus pyramidium** jumping.

they come to the entrance of the burrow and, after much hesitation, make short trips above ground. They gradually gain confidence and eventually start searching for their own food.

Agile enemies

Gerbils are eaten by all kinds of flesh-eating animals including snakes, foxes and shrikes. Their safety lies in being able to dash into a burrow or in jinking. Gerbils are very agile, being able to change direction at each bound, although the bat-eared fox (p. 303) is skilful at out-jumping them. A fat sand rat will often stop at the entrance of its burrow and sit back on its hindlegs to peer at the source of disturbance before disappearing below ground. It would seem better to bolt straight in, and the Indian gerbil has short burrows, distinct from its main burrow, where it can hide when in danger. This gerbil is also said to be able to elude dogs by jumping on their backs and the naked-soled gerbils of Nigeria escape by suddenly leaping to one side and hiding motionless in the cover of grass.

Plague carrier

Gerbil activities sometimes clash with man's interests. They are occasionally a pest to crops or desert reclamation schemes. In Iraq the jird steals grain and stores it in temporary burrows in the fields. Later it removes its booty to permanent stores under stones, where it may be stolen by hamsters. Much more serious pests are the gerbils of South Africa. They are carriers of bubonic plague and unceasing efforts are made to control their numbers.

It is the general rule for small desert animals to come out from their holes at night (see fennec, p 896) but several species of gerbil are diurnal. The fat sand rat can be seen out feeding even during the heat of the afternoon. The intense sunlight in the desert can damage an animal's tissues because some of the radiation is able to penetrate very deep into the body. Nocturnal activity removes this risk. Some observations by a Russian zoologist suggest that the diurnal gerbils are protected from the harmful effects of the sun. The midday jird has very dense fur, with nearly twice as many hairs per square inch as a coypu, which is noted for its thick fur. It also has a thick skin. This is unusual as thick-furred animals usually have thin skins and vice versa. The great gerbil, another diurnal species, has layers of pigment in the skin that prevent the harmful rays from penetrating, whereas the nocturnal gerbils that were studied had no such protection.

class	**Mammalia**
order	**Rodentia**
family	**Cricetidae**
genera & species	***Gerbillus gerbillus*** *pygmy gerbil* ***Meriones meridianus*** *midday jird* ***Psammomys obesus*** *fat sand rat* ***Rhombomys opimus*** *great gerbil* ***Tatera indica*** *Indian gerbil* *others*

Rough but effective: a female gerbil drags her babies to safety after being disturbed. They are helpless until about 3 weeks old.

Gerenuk

Also known as Waller's gazelle or giraffe-necked gazelle, the gerenuk was not set on scientific record until 1878. It is often said that the gerenuk was known to the Ancient Egyptians and was figured in their tombs. In fact only one Egyptian antiquity has been discovered bearing a representation of a long-necked, long-legged antelope and this is more likely to have been the dibatag (see p. 767).

The gerenuk stands up to 41 in. at the shoulder, the length of head, neck and body totals 4½ ft, the tail is 9 in. long and the weight up to 115 lb. The male carries short, thick, lyre-shaped horns up to 17 in. long. The coat is fox red on the back, lighter on the flanks and white below.

Sir Walter Brooke first described the gerenuk from specimens sent to him by a missionary, the Rev Horace Waller, a friend of David Livingstone. Waller had received them from Sir John Kirk, British Consul in Zanzibar, the specimens having come originally from the coast of Somalia. Brooke gave them the name **Gazella walleri.** *An Austrian scientist, Dr Kohl, studied their anatomy and concluded they were not gazelles. One feature he noted was that the skull extended unusually far back behind the horns and that this part was almost solid bone. So he changed the name to* **Lithocranius** *(stony skull)* **walleri,** *but misspelt it* **Litocranius.**

The horizontal position . . .
Gerenuks are excessively shy and readily move away trotting with the head held horizontally forward, so they easily pass under low branches in the thorn bush. A gerenuk when disturbed moves away about 200 yd then stops and raises its head from behind a bush to survey the intruder.

Gerenuks live singly, in pairs or in small herds of 3—10 in the drier parts of southern Ethiopia, Somalia and northern Kenya.

. . . and the vertical
Gerenuks browse foliage, especially acacia, with their long, hairy mobile lips and long tongue. Characteristically a gerenuk will stand on its hindlegs to reach leaves 6 or 7 ft up. They may place the front hooves on the trunks to do this. Where water is available they will drink, but in the drier parts of their range they seem to go long periods without drinking. In the Frankfurt Zoo it has been noticed that gerenuks will drink each other's urine, which may be a means of water conservation in the wild.

Wife-kicking
Although Kohl decided the gerenuk was not a gazelle it has one trick which is seen in Thomson's and Grant's gazelles of East Africa. Before mating the buck throws a front leg forward in the direction of the doe, but instead of inserting it between her hindlegs, as the two gazelles do, he aims it

▷ *Female gerenuk and young.*

Peter Hill

Okania

at her forelegs or flanks. Then he nibbles her muzzle and rubs his head against her, particularly the part of his face just in front of the eye, which is marked with a dark patch. This is the opening of a scent gland, the preorbital gland. In other antelopes it has been found that when the buck's scent is rubbed onto the head and the neck of the doe it brings her more quickly into breeding condition.

There is relatively little information on breeding. Females in zoos had bred for the first time at 19—22 months and, in the wild, the young are born in time to browse the tender new shoots that appear with the rains.

There is no precise information about enemies, but presumably these include any carnivores in their range large enough to take either the kids or the adults. The Somalis refuse to eat the flesh of the gerenuk believing it is a relative of the camel and that if gerenuks are killed, sickness will afflict their camels.

Fauns and satyrs

The most striking thing about the gerenuk is that it can, and habitually does, stand erect on its hindlegs with the neck, back and hindlegs in a straight line. This, however, is not so astonishing as those freak quadrupeds which always walk on two legs. They show how readily an animal can pass from the quadrupedal to the bipedal posture. The most famous of these is known as Slijper's goat.

Professor EJ Slijper wrote in a Dutch scientific journal in 1942 about a he-goat born without forelegs. It lived for a year, and even then only died of an accident. It moved about by jumps on its hindlegs in a semi-upright posture, its body making an angle of 45 degrees with the ground, the hoofs of the hindlegs placed much farther forward than usual to bring them under the centre of gravity.

Buried in various scientific journals in Britain, France, Germany and the USSR are similar accounts of dogs, horses, sheep, goats, cats and other domestic animals born without forelegs or only stumps and compelled to walk erect or nearly so. One dog lived for 12 years despite the handicap.

There is a further interest in this. If this can happen to domesticated animals it could also happen to wild animals. They might not survive so long, especially those like dogs or cats which must hunt for a living. But a herbivore, like a goat, might well survive, and one wonders whether stories of fauns and satyrs may not have sprung from the sight of a bipedal goat. Even the great god Pan may have been nothing more than a Slijper's goat living in classical times.

Full stretch: noses buried in foliage about 7 ft from the ground, a gerenuk couple browse in satyr-like poses.

class	**Mammalia**
order	**Artiodactyla**
family	**Bovidae**
genus & species	*Litocranius walleri*

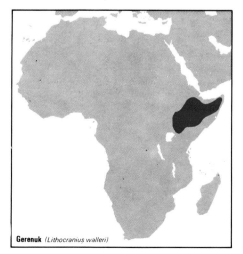

Gerenuk *(Lithocranius walleri)*

1018

German shepherd

The German Shepherd Dog is a breed which may inspire fear or near worship, but seldom indifference. Many people still think that it originates from the wolf, but there is no evidence whatsoever to support this claim.

The German Shepherd has existed in its present form for at least 2000 years – the Egyptian museum in the Louvre, Paris, contains the picture of a dog sculptured in limestone which could easily have had a modern German Shepherd Dog as its model. Much more recent statues sculptured from life are said to have resembled this museum piece to a remarkable degree.

Brains and beauty

Considered by many to be the epitome of brains and beauty in the canine world, the modern German Shepherd Dog owes much of its success, initially, to the work of Captain Reichelman-Dunan and Count Von Hahn. These men recognized the need to improve the working ability and type of German Shepherds generally and joined with other enthusiasts in forming the Phylax Club in order to follow a planned breeding programme to promote such ends. Despite the short life of the Phylax Club (1891–1894) the founders continued to produce a dog which, though much smaller than present specimens, had prick ears, a thick smooth coat and bore a definite resemblance to the dogs we know today.

The most important event in the history of the German Shepherd Dog, however, occurred when Count Von Stephanity (the father of the breed), having long admired certain qualities exhibited by the German herds' dogs, found by chance a dog which so excited his admiration – containing those much admired qualities of intelligence, strength and ability – that he is reputed to have bought it there and then! This dog, Horand V Grafrath – was used as the foundation stone for the German Shepherd breed as we know it today.

The scope of the German Shepherd Dog during the 1914–18 war, as witnessed by soldiers of many nations, caused a surge of popularity. This spread quickly to England and the USA as soldiers began to take dogs home with them. Indeed, when Rin-Tin-Tin (himself born under fire in the trenches and taken as a puppy to the USA) launched himself fearlessly across the cinema screen, he landed fairly and squarely in our hearts. The German Shepherd Dog continued to prove its worth as a guide dog, army dog, police dog, family pet and loyal companion.

A unique breed of dog

Few deny that the German Shepherd Dog is a dog of great personal beauty and symmetry. It covers the ground effortlessly with a smooth and rhythmic stride, presenting a picture of harmonious strength and agility. Its head is noble, cleanly chiselled with a keen, intelligent and composed expression. The large ears, with their distinctive carriage – proud and erect – are possibly one of the reasons why this breed of dog is so often linked with the wolf.

It can give unparalleled pleasure to its owners, but a dog of such acute intelligence must have some kind of 'work' to do. People who purchase a German Shepherd without any thought for the consequences and proceed to neglect it, are those who cause it to be so maligned. Like any bright child, the bored German Shepherd Dog will inevitably turn to mischief. But cared for correctly, it is incorruptible, vigilant and faithful.

Over the last few centuries, many dog breeds have evolved for use in herding and guarding. Most of these breeds have never become known outside their immediate locality. Some, however, because of outstanding attributes such as exceptional intelligence, beauty or adaptability have spread throughout the world. The German Shepherd Dog is one such breed. If a single breed had to be chosen to represent all dogs, then this would surely be the one.

Diane Pearce

Eric Hosking

Gharial

The gharial is a long, slender-snouted crocodile living in the rivers Indus, Ganges and Brahmaputra and in a few other rivers of this same region. The alternative name of gavial, although Latinized to give its scientific name, was originally due to a misspelling. It is now extremely rare and numbers only a few hundred.

The Indian gharial can grow to 20 ft in length. The eyes are set well up on the head and the nostrils are at the tip of the long slender snout. The jaws are armed with small sharp teeth of nearly uniform size. The upper surface of the neck and the back have an armour of bony plates. The legs are longer proportionately than in most other crocodiles and the toes, especially those of the hindfeet, are webbed.

A crocodile very similar to the gharial lives in the rivers and marshes of Malaya, Borneo and Sumatra. Its snout is long but proportionately shorter than that of the gharial, and the two are similar in habits. It is, however, known as the false gharial and is one of the crocodile family (see p. 708) or **Crocodylidae.**

Inoffensive crocodiles

Gharials keep to the water more than other crocodiles. They tend to lie just under the surface with only the eyes and nostrils exposed. When anyone approaches, the eyes sink slowly out of sight, leaving only the nostrils breaking surface. With the closer approach of an intruder the tip of the snout is then submerged. Both gharial and false gharial are little danger to people although there are rare records of fatal encounters. The gharial is sacred to the Hindus, and although its stomach is sometimes found to contain articles of personal adornment, such as bracelets, these have come almost certainly from human corpses committed to the sacred River Ganges.

Handy snout for feeding

The food of the gharial and false gharial is almost entirely small fishes, seized with a sideways snap of the jaws. The slenderness of the snout allows quick movement sideways; it is easier to wave a stick from side to side in water than a plank.

Two-tier incubator

The male gharial has a hollow hump on the tip of the snout with the nostrils at the centre of it. Otherwise there is little outward difference between the sexes. In the breeding season the female lays about 40 eggs in sand on a river bank, each $3\frac{1}{2}$ in. by $2\frac{3}{4}$ in.

△ *Gharial siesta, slumped on a warm bank to make the most of the midday sun.*

These are in 2 layers, probably laid on separate days, and each layer is covered with a fairly deep covering of sand. The newly-hatched young, 14 in. long, have absurdly long snouts and they are coloured greyish-brown with five irregular dark oblique bands on the body and nine on the tail. The adults are mainly dark olive.

Same head, same feeding

Crocodiles in general and their immediately recognisable ancestors have a very long history going back over 200 million years. The crocodiles proper, living today, which must include also the caimans and alligators, do not differ much from their earliest ancestors, except that some of the extinct crocodiles are larger than the largest living today. There was, however, a separate group of crocodilians whose fossils also date from those very early times, known as the Mesosuchia. They also had 'frying-pan' heads like the gharials, but they lived in the sea and they died out 120 million years ago. The gharials came into existence much later, less than 70 million years ago, and one of them was 54 ft long, the largest crocodilian we know of, living or extinct.

The Mesosuchia and the gharials are,

apart from being members of the order Crocodilia, not related. But they both had the long slender snout and both had many small sharp teeth. They both had the same feeding habits, seizing fast-moving slippery prey with a sideways slash of the head. We know gharials do this because people have watched the living animals feeding. We know false gharials do also, for the same reason, and we can deduce the Mesosuchia did this from the finer details of their bones. So we have three kinds of crocodilians with the same shape of head, feeding in the same way but all three unrelated. We know the gharials snatch fish; we can deduce the Mesosuchia snatched squid.

Many animals have pebbles in their stomachs. Living crocodiles are one example. Extinct crocodiles are another, and we know this because when their skeletons are dug out of the ground groups of pebbles are found lying where the stomach would have been.

How do we know the Mesosuchia ate squid? Because the stomach stones found where their stomachs would have been are stained with the ink contained in the bodies of squids.

class	**Reptilia**
order	**Crocodilia**
family	**Gavialidae**
genus & species	***Gavialis gangeticus***

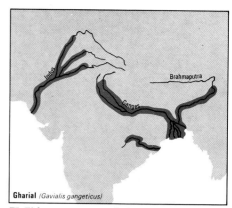

Gharial *(Gavialis gangeticus)*

▽ *Fish trap: once caught in this array of vicious teeth by a sideways slash of the gharial's head, few fish, slimy or not, can escape.*

Ghost frog

The ghost frog of South Africa gets its name from the white skin of its underside, which is so thin that the digestive organs are visible through it. Its back is green, marked with a reddish network. Compared with other frogs, its body is small relative to the head and unusually long legs, and there is almost a suggestion of a neck. The head is flattish with the eyes more prominent than is usual in frogs, and the toes of all four feet end in discs. When an animal species is placed first in one family, then in another, it usually means that its relationship with other animals is not clear. Some scientists put the ghost frogs in a family of their own, the Heleophrynidae, others put them in the Leptodactylidae, but all leading authorities now agree on the latter. The animals normally end up in a genus of their own. This is true of the ghost frogs, of which there are three species. One species **Heleophryne rosei** *lives on Table Mountain, another* **H. purcelli** *is found in Cape Province, and the third* **H. natalensis** *is in the Transvaal and Natal. The frogs are elusive in another way: they are very hard to find, but the real reason for their name is that you can almost see through them.*

John Visser

The ghost frog gets its name from the white skin of its underside. It is very difficult to track down and as a result is rarely seen. This may be partially explained by the fact that it is nocturnal — as shown by its diamond-shaped pupils formed during daylight to keep out bright light.

Equipped for climbing

Ghost frogs have toes shaped like those of tree frogs, although they climb little. Instead, they tend to spend the day crouching in holes in the ground, under stones or in caves, and they also spend much of their time in water. At night they come out and clamber over large rocks or into trees. Another unusual feature is that the skin of the undersides of the forelimbs and the tops of the fingers has groups of small hooks, and similar hooks form a double row on either side along the lower jaw with scattered hooks on the upper jaw and the snout. It has been suggested that these help the frog to cling to the surfaces of slippery rocks. This description applies to the best known of the ghost frogs, *Heleophryne rosei*. Another species also has spines on the skin, and this one climbs into bushes.

Mainly insect-eaters

Frogs shed their skins periodically and in most species the frog eats the cast skin, which is sloughed more or less in one piece. Ghost frogs shed their skins in pieces and make no attempt to eat them. It should be emphasized, however, that in this as in everything else concerned with their biology we have only a small amount of information. Ghost frogs are difficult to track down and are rarely seen. Possibly part of the explanation is seen in their eyes, diamond-shaped with the long axis of the diamond vertical — an unusual eye, showing nocturnal habits.

Ghost frogs probably eat insects, and one species *H. purcelli* has been seen capturing flies by leaping up at them.

Holding on to food

By dissecting the dead female ghost frog it is known that she lays about 30 large eggs. Where she does this is not known, and the guess is that she lays them in a hole in a river bank just above water level. More is known about the tadpoles which are somewhat flattened, especially in the head. Seen from above they are wedge-shaped except for the tail. Around the mouth is a large sucker by which the tadpole can cling to submerged rocks and browse the small algae on their surfaces.

Mountain chicken — frogs of the West Indies

Those not versed in field natural history may wonder why, once a species is known to exist, somebody does not set to work to learn all about it. To illustrate the difficulties we cannot do better than tell the story of the mountain chicken of the West Indies. This is a frog *Leptodactylus fallax* which belongs to the same family as the ghost frogs if we accept the majority view. It is nearly 6 in. long, weighs up to 2 lb and lives on the islands of Dominica, Montserrat and Martinique. The frog lives in the steep-sided valleys which are heavily forested and difficult of access. During the day, so far as anyone can tell, it rests in burrows in the ground or in cavities among boulders. The females have never been seen and nothing is known of the way they breed. They do not live near streams, so possibly they make foam nests in the trees like related species living in South America are known to do. The males come out at night and call

with a musical, bird-like 'song', but the reason why they are called mountain chicken is that the flesh of their legs cooked with egg and bread crumbs is delicious, like the best chicken. The frog has been almost eliminated from Martinique, partly because introduced mongooses have preyed on them and partly because they are much prized for the table.

An English zoologist visiting Dominica tried to find the females in the hope of studying the life history of the species. He found some of the males, but even this entailed climbing the steep slopes at night in rain, negotiating tangles of tree roots, creepers and boulders, finding his way by electric torch and guided by the somewhat ventriloquial musical calls of the males, which go on singing all night. Even to find a few males was a small reward for all the effort and discomfort he expended. The males themselves do not help because they tend to sit near the mouth of a burrow or cavity among the boulders into which they can readily retreat.

After all, if you can only find males your knowledge of a species must be very incomplete. And if you eat those males it cannot be long before a population of spinster frogs is created — and that means the end of the species.

class	**Amphibia**
order	**Salientia**
family	**Leptodactylidae**
genus	*Heleophryne natalensis* *H. purcelli* *H. rosei*

Giant forest hog

This forest hog, the largest wild pig in the world, very nearly became extinct before the western world ever knew about it. It was unknown to Europeans until 1904 when a skull and pieces of skin were given to Colonel Richard Meinertzhagen by the local hunters of the Kakamega Forest in western Kenya. Since then it has been found on Mount Kenya, in the Aberdare Mountains and in the mountain forests of Uganda and westwards through Zaire to Liberia.

A large boar may be 5 ft long with a 13 in. tail, 3 ft high at the shoulder and weigh up to 600 lb. The body is thickset, the head broad and stout, the clay-coloured skin covered with long black bristles. The snout is heavy, with large upper tusks growing out at right angles. The skin in front of the eye is naked, and behind each eye is a pair of warts. These are much the same as the warts on the face of the more ugly warthog but their position and shape is different — and nobody knows what they are for. On the naked skin in front of the eye is a slit, the entrance to a facial scent gland which no other pig has. Another unusual feature is that on the top of the head is a deep depression 'large enough to take a tangerine orange', as one French zoologist put it.

Pig with clean habits

Forest hogs, shy and retiring, move about in groups or 'sounders' of 4–20 in dense undergrowth of rain forests, where they have their runs and bedding-down places. They also frequent swampy places to wallow. They seldom use a burrow and even less do they construct one, but they dig holes at the bases of trees to use as latrines. Their usual habit is to keep well out of sight but old boars brought to bay by dogs or wounded can be dangerous. They have also been known to attack humans in defence of the sounder.

Little more is known about them except that they feed mainly on lush grass and shrubs, and unlike most species of wild pig do not root in the ground for food. They come out of the dense undergrowth in the early morning to feed, and again in the late afternoon and evening. The litters may contain 2–6 young, born after a gestation of 125 days.

Tracking it down

The story of why so little is known about these giant hogs is one of the most romantic in the annals of large mammals. Several of the early explorers in Central Africa, including Sir Henry Stanley as well as Sir Harry Johnston, who discovered the okapi, had heard stories about it from the Africans but none had been able to see it. Then, in 1903, Colonel (then Lieutenant) Richard Meinertzhagen, a professional soldier, since famous as a naturalist and author of books on birds, heard about it when he was in Kenya. He determined to find it but bad luck dogged him. First he heard one had

A sounder of giant forest hogs on a night feeding expedition. A sounder is made up of 4–20 hogs. The largest wild pig in the world, a large boar may be 5 ft long and over 600 lb in weight.

been killed by African hunters but by the time he had reached the spot the carcase had been carved up and all he could get were two pieces of the skin. A little while later he heard of another having been killed. This time he got some of the skin and also the skull. These few relics, and especially the skull, were enough to show the animal belonged to an unnamed species, so Meinertzhagen sent them to London where they were shown to the Fellows of the Zoological Society. An account of them was published in that Society's Proceedings for 1904.

The pig that nearly died out

In following years several more skulls as well as drawings of the animal were sent to the Natural History Museum in London. Occasionally white hunters in Central Africa had a sight of it, and people who visited Tree Tops, the famous look-out in Kenya, were sometimes able to see it. All the same, the giant forest hog is one of the rarer animals. So far as it has been possible to piece the story together it seems that it used to be much more numerous. Then, in 1891, the disease known as rinderpest swept across Africa and the giant forest hog suffered so badly that it is now rare.

Colonel R Meinertzhagen who tracked the hog.

Fact and fable

Many of the stories told to the early explorers by the Africans were highly coloured as to the hog's ferocity. This was the natural reaction to being attacked unawares. For example, the women going into the forest to gather firewood were sometimes ambushed. Although some of the estimates of its size given by the Africans proved accurate, others were often badly exaggerated. This also is the reaction of people everywhere to mystery animals. Nevertheless, there could in this instance be some justification, for, as as result of Dr LSB Leakey's discoveries in Kenya in the last 20 years, we now know there used to be giant animals in that part of Africa, including hogs the size of a rhinoceros or hippopotamus.

class	**Mammalia**
order	**Artiodactyla**
family	**Suidae**
genus & species	*Hylochoerus meinertzhageni*

The distribution of the hog is localised.

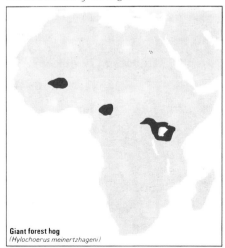

Giant forest hog
(Hylochoerus meinertzhageni)

Giant rat

Some rats are little bigger than mice, but others are nearly 3 ft long and have deservedly been called giant rats. A few not quite as long as this have been called giant rats, but one that deserves the title is the African giant pouched rat, also called the Gambian pouched rat. It is found from Gambia in the west to the Sudan and Kenya in the east and southwards to the Transvaal. It is nearly 3 ft long of which just over half is tail. Its fur may be sleek or harsh, grey to brown on the back, lighter on the flanks and whitish on the underparts, with the feet and legs noticeably white or pink. Some are mottled, almost spotted. The head is long and narrow and the ears large. The tail is naked.

The Gambian, pouched or African giant rat, numerous over so wide an area, has many local names, in the African languages as well as in English. In Sierra Leone it is the ground pig, in Ghana the bush rat. In northern Nigeria it is the bandicoot and in western Nigeria the rabbit.

Short-sighted giant

The African giant rat lives in the rain forests of west central Africa, in the bush, on farms, in grassland, under piles of logs, even on the summits of the huge bare rocks, known as insulbergs, standing in the savannah. It is solitary, living in a burrow that may have 2–6 entrances, and it is said these are often closed from the inside with leaves. Mainly active at night, it may sometimes be seen by day sitting on its haunches, sniffing in all directions as if blind, despite its bright eyes, and it can be seen doing exactly the same at night. This suggests it is very short-sighted and doubtless depends mainly on its nose and, more especially, its large ears, which are constantly on the move. When running it holds its tail well up. It is wholly inoffensive and docile, and can be picked up by the tail and handled without fear of its biting. When not feeding it keeps up a constant bird-like chirping.

Built-in shopping bags

The food of the giant rat is any plant material, especially grain, fruits and nuts. It is called the pouched rat from its capacious cheek-pouches, which have earned it the additional name of hamster rat. It stuffs these pouches with food until its face is twice the normal size, then runs away and, working the food forwards with its paws, spits it out in a heap to store it.

Pink and white rats

The breeding season seems to vary from one part of its range to another. Usually 2–3 young are born at a time after a gestation of about 42 days. They are pink and white at first, the body and head about 4 in. long with a tail half as long again. Brown fur begins to show at about 3 weeks.

African 'small beef'

Little is known of natural enemies but they must include almost any local beast or bird of prey. Their greatest enemy is probably man, since the Africans regard their flesh as a delicacy and dig the giant rats out of their burrows. To them the flesh is 'small beef'.

Many island giants

By contrast with the giant pouched rat the five species of giant naked-tailed rat, or African big-toothed mouse *Uranomys*, only 8½ in. long overall and covering much the same range, are all rare. They are hardly worthy of the name of giant. For really big rats we need to go farther west, to the islands of the Indo-Pacific. The New Guinea giant tree rat *Mallomys rothschildi* lives among rocks 4–8 thousand ft up and feeds on plants, especially fern shoots. It is 34 in. overall with thick woolly brown to grey fur, a scaly tail and long curved claws. Another New Guinea giant rat is *Hyomys goliath*, grey with light underparts and also nearly 3 ft total length. Little is known of the habits of either of these giants. A third species on New Guinea is the giant naked-tailed rat *Uromys caudimaculatus*, 28 in. long, of which half is tail, and there are species related to it on the islands of Aru and Kei, of the Bismarck Archipelago and the Solomons, as well as in Queensland, Australia. Again little is known about them. There is a giant tree rat *Papagomys armandvillei* on the island of Flores of which practically nothing is known and very few specimens have been obtained. On the island of Luzon, in the Philippines, are two species of cloud rat, both nearly 3 ft long, one of them with a bushy tail, and this one is trapped by the aboriginal inhabitants of the island and their pelts sold in the markets. Yet we are in almost complete ignorance of how they live. There are three species of giant water rat: one in New Guinea, one in New Britain and the third in Australia and Tasmania and also on a number of the islands to the north of Australia. A little more is known about

Giant rat or Gambian pouched rat youngster stuffs its food pouches with food. It will push in fruit, grain and nuts until its face is twice the normal size before going off to store it.

Jane Burton. Photo Res

these, but still not very much. They are nocturnal, sleeping by day in a burrow in the bank, a hollow log or under a pile of vegetable litter, and they feed on water snails, mussels, fish, frogs and water birds. They have a long flattened head, eyes set high up on the head, small ears and seal-like fur and their feet are partially webbed. Starting in 1937 they were extensively trapped in Australia for their fur and now they have to be protected.

class	**Mammalia**
order	**Rodentia**
family	**Muridae**
genus & species	***Cricetomys gambianus*** *others*

◁ *Baby giant rat.*
▽ *Cocoa bean investigation: this giant rat may be eaten by Africans who regard its flesh as a delicacy—to them it is 'small beef'.*

Giant snail

A pest in many parts of the world, **Achatina achatina** *is a large land-living snail, native to West Africa. With its pointed shell, 5 or even 8 in. long, it weighs about ½ lb. This species deserves the title of giant snail, although there are other large terrestrial snails in many of the warmer countries, because of its notoriety and economic importance. The fact that even larger snails live in the sea seems somehow less remarkable.*

In other respects, there is little of note in the appearance of the giant snail as compared with the snails of our gardens.

Dusk feeder

The giant snail feeds mainly by night or at dusk, usually returning after its forays to a regular 'home'. However, it will also come out by day if there is rain or if the sky is overcast. For continued activity, dampness and a temperature above about 24°C/75°F are needed. On the other hand, during dry or cold periods it remains inactive, often deep in some hollow log or under a rock and withdrawn into its shell, the aperture closed off with a thin membrane. This state of inactivity, or aestivation as it is called, has been known to last for as long as a year —a long enough time, but not to be compared with the 6 years recorded for an individual of another species of snail. When so much time can be spent in suspended animation, records of longevity have little meaning, but one specimen is recorded as having lived 9 years in captivity.

A taste for whitewash

To a large extent the giant snail feeds on rotten plant matter and dead animals but it will also feed voraciously on the leaves, fruit, bark and flowers of a great variety of plants—including, unfortunately, crops like beans, breadfruit, cabbage, cacao, citrus trees, melons, yam plants and rubber. Needing calcium to form its shell, it may even climb walls of houses to ravage the whitewash on them for its lime content.

Pea-sized eggs

These giant snails begin breeding when about a year old and, like their smaller relatives, are hermaphrodite. They lay eggs the size of small peas, like miniature bird's eggs with lemon-yellow shells. These they deposit, 40–500 at a time, in or on the soil, doing so every 2 or 3 months. The young hatch in 1–10 days. A single snail can apparently lay eggs without mating after months of isolation, for evidently sperm can be stored for this time before being used. One result is that a single snail can suffice to found a new colony if it was fertilised before being transported.

Growth of a pest

In its East African home, the giant snail is hardly a pest, but it has spread from there to many of the warmer parts of the world, becoming in most of them a considerable pest. Like the rabbit in Australia,

it is one of too many examples of animals or plants, originally fairly innocuous, that have become pests outside their native lands. Everything about this snail, such as its ability to eat almost any plant material and its high rate of reproduction, combined with its hardiness and a scarcity of natural enemies, favour its chances of colonising new areas, provided that the climate is suitable. Just a few individuals need be introduced—even one is enough.

The spread of the giant snail started in about 1800 when some were taken to Mauritius by the wife of the governor on doctor's orders (medicinal properties have been ascribed to these snails as to others). There they multiplied and became a pest. Some were taken to the island of Réunion and to the Seychelles and, in 1847, some were released in Calcutta. From then on the snail has appeared in more and more countries—particularly in the Indo-Pacific area, including Malaya, Indonesia, the Philippines, Thailand, Vietnam, and China.

Jane Burton: Photo Res

This West African giant snail has a pointed shell 5–8 in. long and weighs about ½ lb. Introduction into many parts of the world mainly for its food value has resulted in it becoming a pest.

Sometimes introductions have been accidental, the snails being transported while aestivating in bananas, in soil, or in motor vehicles. Sometimes they have been deliberately introduced. In 1928, for instance, they were introduced to Sarawak to be used as poultry feed and in 1936 to the Hawaiian islands by a lady wishing to keep two in her garden as pets. The Japanese forces took them as food for themselves into New Guinea and elsewhere and, before the Second World War, they were eaten by Malays and by Chinese in various places. Other related giant snails are important as food in parts of West Africa. In Ghana they are the greatest single source of animal protein. The value of snails as food, however, even to those willing to eat them, is

more than offset by the damage they can inflict on crops and gardens, for they can occur in huge numbers, like apples under an apple tree.

The nuisance does not end there, for in places the ground may become slippery with slime, excreta and dead snails, and roads in Sri Lanka and Saipan have been turned into 'stinking nightmares' as more and more were attracted to their crushed fellows. Worse still, the slimy mess provides breeding grounds for disease-bearing flies. With others dying in drinking wells, devouring with impunity the warfarin bait and springing the traps put out for rats, it is hardly surprising that much effort is devoted to their control. Poisons have been used as well as various predators—including other carnivorous snails—but always there is the danger in these methods of upsetting the balance of nature in yet other ways, such as the controlling predators attacking innocuous species, and so becoming pests themselves. The best method of all,

if it can be used in time, is a rigorous system of control to prevent the spread of the snail. It is encouraging that, in some areas, after an initial heavy infestation, the population diminishes to a steady level at which they are not such serious pests.

phylum	**Mollusca**
class	**Gastropoda**
order	**Stylommatophora**
family	**Achatinidae**
genus & species	***Achatina fulica*** *East Africa* ***A. achatina*** *West Africa*

Gibbon

The most agile of mammals and smallest of the five apes (including man) the gibbon is distinguished by its extremely long arms, which may be 1½ times the length of the legs. Most gibbons are about 3 ft high when standing upright, but the largest species, the siamang, reaches 4 ft. The fingers are long and the thumbs appear long because they are deeply cleft from the palms of the hands. The thumbs are also very mobile and gibbons are adept at manipulating objects. The nails are clawlike and the fangs, which in other apes are long in the males and short in females, are long in both male and female gibbons. As the males are only slightly larger than the females, the sexes tend to look alike except for their colour.

The six species of gibbon live in southeast Asia from Assam south to Java. The siamang lives in Malaya and Sumatra and the dwarf siamang lives on some small islands west of Sumatra. The species differ in colour. The siamangs are entirely black. The males of the concolor, hoolock and black-capped gibbons are black and the females fawn. Both sexes of these gibbons are whitish when born, turning black in their first year. At maturity the males remain black while the females turn fawn. The sixth species, the lar gibbon, the one most often seen in zoos, has several races. The white-handed and agile races of Malaya and Sumatra have light and dark colour phases, independent of sex. The silvery gibbon of Java and Borneo is uniformly grey or brown. The concolor gibbon differs in that the male has a crest of hair.

Superb acrobats

Gibbons live high in the trees, where they travel by swinging by their arms. They are popular in zoos for the way they will swing from one end of the cage to the other, grabbing bars with their hands and throwing themselves forwards without a check in their progression. Their agility is quite incredible, as they make apparently effortless leaps of 30 ft or more, and their reflexes match it. A gibbon was once seen to jump from a branch just as it broke, and so fail to get enough momentum to reach the next branch. Twisting in mid-air, the gibbon grabbed the stump of the broken branch, swung right around it and flew off to its destination. The gibbon's agility is mainly due to its long arms, which can move freely in all directions, its light body and the long fingers that are held in a hooked position with the thumbs out of the way. Gibbons are also agile on the ground. Apart from man, they are the only apes that

▷ *Overleaf: The ability to swing hand over hand is the art of the gibbon. Its wrist, long arm and shoulder are adapted for this movement, known as brachiation.*
▷ *Almost human: a silvery gibbon stands erect.*

habitually walk upright on their hindlegs. When walking on the ground or along a branch, they hold their arms out to help in balancing.

Other apes are becoming rare, but the gibbon is still quite numerous in the wild; soldiers returning from Vietnam often brought home pet gibbons. They are not the best of pets, the females in particular being liable to fits of bad temper, but the males usually become tame and affectionate.

Gibbons live in small groups, often a pair with up to four offspring. Each group owns a small territory varying from 40 to 300 acres. They sleep in the centre of the territory, huddled together on a branch, squatting on their ischial callosities, or sitting pads—hard patches of skin on their rumps. Gibbons probably mate for life and they are very aggressive to other gibbons. Each morning some, usually the females, begin calling, uttering the 'great-call' which is used as an advertisement. This attracts the groups towards each other and they often meet at the boundaries of their territories. The males leap about uttering the 'conflict-call', a series of hoots, and eventually one male may chase another, forcing him back into his own territory, then rapidly retreating. Very occasionally there is a fight and the two males scratch and bite each other. After an hour or so the conflicts die down and the groups wander back into their territories to feed.

Each species of gibbon has a very characteristic great-call, by which it can be recognised even if the gibbons are hidden in the tree canopy. The black-capped gibbon has the most musical call consisting of a rising crescendo of wistful-sounding whoops followed by a rapidly descending series. The hoolock gibbons produce a call that is imitated by the name. It is stimulated by another gibbon calling or by a sudden change in the weather such as a shower of rain or the appearance of the sun. The siamang has a special throat pouch. Filling it produces a deep resonant boom, followed by a harsh, honking exhalation, which can be heard over a wide area.

Snatching birds from the air

Gibbons eat mostly fruit, such as figs, grapes and mangoes. They also eat leaves, insects, eggs and occasionally birds, which they have been seen catching in mid-air as they leap from one branch to another. In the tropical forests a group of gibbons can usually find all the food it requires within its territory as the trees fruit all the year round. Occasionally, however, the trees along the boundary are disputed with the neighbours.

Breeding all the year round

Gibbons breed all the year round. A single baby is born after a 7-month gestation. At first it is helpless and is carried, clasped to the mother's breast. A few weeks later it begins to take an interest in its surroundings and is carried clinging around its mother's waist like a belt. When she is swinging through the trees she raises her legs to give the baby extra support and protection. After weaning, the baby joins in the social life of its family. Mature at 6 years old, gibbons live to about 25 years.

Photo Researchers

Smallest but the most successful ape, a gibbon hangs by a hand. The hands have long fingers and the thumbs appear long because they are deeply cleft from the palms of the hand.

Not so dim

Gibbons are often said to be the least intelligent of apes, but recent tests have shown that they may be as intelligent as chimpanzees. The reason for the gibbons' supposed lack of intelligence was that they were not so adept at problem-solving tests as the other apes. The tests are absurdly simple for a man. Food such as a banana is placed out of reach beyond the bars of the apes' cage. A piece of string is tied to the banana and led to the bars. The ape has no trouble pulling the string to get its banana but the situation is made more difficult by having two pieces of string. One, for instance, may run straight from banana to cage, but pulling it does not draw the banana nearer, while the other runs first away from the cage then back, and is the right one to pull to get the banana. The ape can solve the problem by trial-and-error, pulling strings at random until it gets the right one, or by insight, that is by working out the problem in its head.

Gibbons were apparently unable to solve these problems, but it seems that they were unfairly set. The strings ran along the ground and gibbons had difficulty in grasping them. If, however, the strings are raised, the gibbons, being adapted for hanging on to branches or vines, could take hold of them. This is a point of great importance in designing tests of an animal's intelligence. It has to be able to carry out the necessary movements. For example, it would be no good expecting a dog to pull a suspended string with its paws. Using the improved tests it was found that gibbons could solve the problems as well as other apes. First they would pull the wrong string, and give up and climb round the cage. Then, suddenly, they would return and without hesitation pull the right string. Apparently they had been thinking about the problem and worked it out.

class	**Mammalia**
order	**Primates**
family	**Pongidae**
genera & species	***Hylobates concolor*** *concolor gibbon*
	H. hoolock *hoolock gibbon*
	H. lar *lar gibbon*
	H. pileatus *black-capped gibbon*
	Symphalangus syndactylus *siamang*
	S. klossii *dwarf siamang*

Beringer & Pampaluchi: Bavaria

Geoffrey Kinns

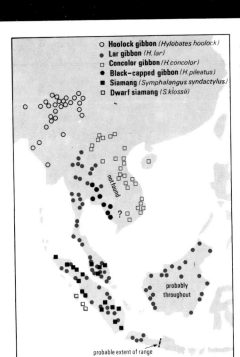

○ **Hoolock gibbon** *(Hylobates hoolock)*
● **Lar gibbon** *(H. lar)*
□ **Concolor gibbon** *(H. concolor)*
● **Black-capped gibbon** *(H. pileatus)*
■ **Siamang** *(Symphalangus syndactylus)*
□ **Dwarf siamang** *(S. klossii)*

not found

?

probably
throughout

probable extent of range

At home with the gibbons

*A 6 day old gibbon clings instinctively to its
mother (above). The mother will lavish intense
care on her offspring until it is weaned.
Portrait of a lar gibbon (above centre). The
eyes are designed for binocular vision. They
are forward directing giving overlapping sight
which enables the gibbon to focus accurately on
branches it is aiming for in its aerial
acrobatic movements (above right).
Siamang family (right). The siamang is the
largest of the six gibbon species with an arm-
spread of as much as 5 ft. It has a throat sac
which can be inflated to about the size of its
head when a call is given. This call has been
described as the combined bark of a dog and the
hoot of a grouse. In the early morning all the
members of a family give a short 'concert',
hooting in unison for several minutes. This
noise carries for considerable distances—
often over two miles. The map marks (left)
show the positions of recorded specimens.
Apart from the siamang which is rather
different from the others, the species of gibbon
have separate ranges which overlap only
slightly so there is no real competition.*

If looks could kill: massive-headed, belly-dragging, obese and ugly, the Gila monster is among the more repulsive of reptiles and one of the only two poisonous lizards. Surprisingly, many people have kept it as a pet; enough, in fact, to make it rare. It is now protected by law.

Gila monster

Only two out of about 3 000 kinds of lizards are poisonous: the Gila monster (pronounced 'heela') and the beaded lizard. They look alike and live in deserts of the southwestern United States and adjacent parts of Mexico respectively. The first is named for the Gila basin in Arizona where it is plentiful, the second after the beaded nature of its scales.

The Gila monster is up to 23 in. long and weighs up to 3¼ lb. It is mainly pink and yellow with black shading. The beaded lizard, up to 32 in. long, is mainly black with pink and yellow patches. The Gila monster has 4—5 dark bands on the tail. The beaded lizard has 6—7 yellow bands. Both have a stout body, large blunt head, powerful lower jaw, small eyes, an unusually thick tail, short legs with 5 toes on each and remarkably strong claws.

Alternate gluttony and fasting

These lizards move about very slowly, although when captured they can move swiftly and struggle actively, hissing all the while. They spend long periods of time in their burrows in the sand, coming out at the rainy season and even then mainly at night. Being slow movers they must eat things that

cannot run away. These are mainly eggs of birds and other reptiles, baby birds and baby mice and rats. They track them down partly by smell but more especially by taste, using the tongue to pick up scent particles on the sand from birds' nests or rodents' burrows. These are conveyed by the tongue to Jacobson's organ, a sort of taste-smell organ in the roof of the mouth. They eat insects and earthworms in captivity and from the behaviour of these captive animals it seems unlikely that venom is used to kill prey. Eggs are either seized, the head raised and the shell crushed so the contents flow into the mouth, or bitten in two and the tongue used to lap up the contents as the shell lies on the ground. The Gila monster drinks liquid food by lapping it up and holding its head back to let the liquid run down its tongue.

While active these lizards eat all they can find and store the surplus as fat in the body and especially in the tail. When well-fed their skeleton represents a small part of the total weight of the body and the lizards can then survive long periods of fasting. The fat tail will then shrink to ⅕ its former girth and the rest of the body will be little more than skin and bone. The lizard will quickly recover once it can find food. One that had survived three years drought, during which it took no food, was taken into captivity and in 6 months its tail had doubled in size and the body was as plump as usual.

Inefficient venom apparatus

The venom glands are in the lower jaw although teeth in both jaws are grooved. Each gland has several ducts that open into a groove between the lower lip and the gum, and the poison finds its way from this to the grooves in the teeth. Neither of the lizards can strike as a snake does but must hold with the teeth and hang on with a vice-like grip sometimes chewing to help conduct the venom. If bitten by a monster, the main problem is to free the tight-gripping jaws.

Nests in the sand

Mating takes place in July and eggs are laid a few weeks later. These are laid in a hole dug by the female with her front feet and covered with sand. There may be 3—15 in a clutch, each egg about 1½ by 2½ in. and oval, with a tough leathery shell. They hatch in about a month, the young lizards being 3½—4¾ in. long, and more vivid in colour than the parents.

Legally protected monster

Little is known of the natural enemies of the two poisonous lizards but by 1952 the Gila monster was becoming so rare it had to be protected by law to save it from extinction. It was being caught and sold in large numbers as a pet. Those who caught them were paid 25—50 cents an inch, and the lizards were then sold at 1—2 dollars an inch.

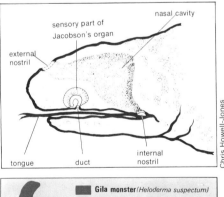

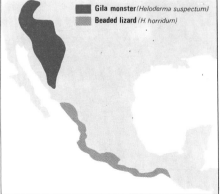

Lizard with a bad name

In striking contrast with the popularity of the Gila monster as a pet are many erroneous beliefs that have gathered around it in the past. One is that it cannot eliminate body wastes, which is why it is so poisonous. For the same reason its breath is evil-smelling. Another is that it can spit venom, whereas at most, when hissing, it may spray a little venom. The lizard has been credited also with leaping on its victims, largely the result perhaps of the way it will lash out from side to side when held in the hand. Its tongue has been said to be poisonous, the lizard itself impossible to kill and possessed of magical powers. Lastly, it has been said to be a cross between a lizard and a crocodile.

More than 400 years ago, a Spaniard, Francisco Hernández, wrote that the bite of the lizard though harmful was not fatal, that it threatened no harm except when provoked and that its appearance was more to be dreaded than its bite. Although his writings had been overlooked the first scientists to study it seem to have taken much the same view when they named it *Heloderma suspectum*, because they were not sure whether it was poisonous, only suspected of being so. They were more certain about the beaded lizard which they named *H. horridum*. Now we know that the poison is a neurotoxin which causes swelling, loss of consciousness, vomiting, palpitations, laboured breathing,

dizziness, a swollen tongue and swollen glands. Not all these symptoms appear in one person, however. The swelling and the initial pain are due to the way the poison is injected. The lizard must hold on and chew with a sideways action of the teeth.

In 1956 Charles M Bogert and Rafael Martin del Campo published in America the results of their thoroughgoing investigation into the injuries suffered by human beings from the bite of the Gila monster. They found only 34 known cases of which 8 were said to have been fatal. Most of those who had died were either in poor health at the time or drunk. In several instances there were signs of repeated biting, as in the case of the man who carried the lizard inside his shirt, next to his skin. This may explain the drunks who fell victim. They teased the lizards in zoos and probably did not realise they were being repeatedly bitten.

△ *Lizard connoisseur: using tongue and 'nose', a Gila monster tests its surroundings.*

▽ *Section through Gila monster's head, showing Jacobson's organ in the roof of the mouth. This is a specialised organ of smell, supplementing or replacing the nose. Scent particles are picked up and conveyed to it by the tongue.*

class	**Reptilia**
order	**Squamata**
suborder	**Sauria**
family	**Helodermatidae**
genus & species	*Heloderma horridum* beaded lizard *H. suspectum* Gila monster

Günter Senfft

Chris Howell-Jones

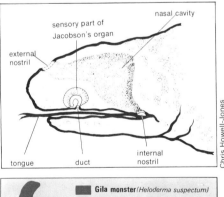

sensory part of Jacobson's organ

nasal cavity

external nostril

internal nostril

tongue

duct

Gila monster *(Heloderma suspectum)*
Beaded lizard *(H. horridum)*

The lofty ones

Dappled freaks of the African veld: a group of giraffes rear their extraordinary necks against the skyline of a pale sunset.

Giraffe

Tallest animal in the world, the giraffe is remarkable for its long legs and long neck. An old bull may be 18 ft to the top of his head. Females are smaller. The head tapers to mobile hairy lips, the tongue is extensile and the eyes are large. There are 2–5 horns, bony knobs covered with skin, including one pair on the forehead, a boss in front, and, in some races, a small pair farther back. The shoulders are high and the back slopes down to a long tufted tail. The coat is boldly spotted and irregularly blotched chestnut, dark brown or liver-coloured on a pale buff ground, giving the effect of a network of light-coloured lines. A number of species and races have been recognized in the past, differing mainly in details of colour and number of horns, but the current view is that all belong to one species. The number of races recognised, however, varies between 8 and 13 species depending on the authority.

The present-day range of the giraffe is the dry savannah and semi-desert of Africa south of the Sahara although it was formerly more widespread. Its range today is from Sudan and Somalia south to South Africa and westwards to northern Nigeria. In many parts of its former range it has been wiped out for its hide.

A leisurely anarchy

Giraffes live in herds with a fairly casual social structure. It seems that males live in groups in forested zones, the old males often solitary, and the females and young live apart from them in more open country. Males visit these herds mainly for mating.

Giraffes do not move about much, and tend to walk at a leisurely pace unless disturbed. When walking slowly the legs move in much the same way as those of a horse. That is, the right hindleg touches the ground just after the right foreleg leaves it, and a little later the left legs make the same movement. The body is therefore supported on three legs most of the time while walking. As the pace quickens to a gallop the giraffe's leg movements change to the legs on each side moving forward together, the two right hoofs hitting the ground together followed by the two left legs moving together.

The long neck not only allows a giraffe to browse high foliage, the eyes set on top of the high head form a sort of watch-tower to look out for enemies. In addition, the long neck and heavy head assist movement by acting as a counterpoise. When resting crouched, with legs folded under the body the neck may be held erect or, if sleeping, the giraffe lays its neck along its back. To rise, the forelegs are half-unfolded, the neck being swung back to take the weight off the forequarters. Then it is swung forwards to take the weight off the hindlegs, for them to be unfolded. By repeated movements of this kind the animal finally gets to its feet.

Adult giraffes apparently sleep little: not at all according to some authors, one-half hour in 24 according to others.

Necking parties

The habit of 'necking' has been something of a puzzle. Two giraffes stand side-by-side and belabour each other with their heads, swinging their long necks slowly and forcibly. Only rarely does any injury result, and the necking seems to be a ritualized fighting, to establish dominance, and confined exclusively, or nearly so, to the male herds.

Not so dumb

One long-standing puzzle concerns the voice. For a long time everyone accepted the idea that giraffes are mute—yet they have an unusually large voice-box. During the last 25 years it has been found that a young giraffe will bleat like the calf of domestic cattle, that the adult female makes a sound like 'wa-ray' and that adult bulls, and sometimes cows, will make a husky grunt or cough. Nevertheless, there are many zookeepers who have never heard a giraffe utter a call and there is still the puzzle why there should be such a large voice-box when so little use is made of it. Some zoologists have suggested the giraffe may use ultrasonics.

Controlled blood pressure

In feeding, leaves are grasped with the long tongue and mobile lips. Trees and bushes tend to become hourglass-shaped from giraffes browsing all round at a particular level. Acacia is the main source of food but many others are browsed, giraffes showing definite preferences for some species of trees or bushes over others.

Giraffes drink regularly when water is available but can go long periods without drinking. They straddle the front legs widely to bring the head down to water, or else straddle them slightly and then bend them at the knees. Another long-standing puzzle concerns the blood pressure in the head, some zoologists maintaining a giraffe must lower and raise its head slowly to prevent a rush of blood to the head. In fact, the blood vessels have valves, reservoirs of blood in the head and alternative routes for the blood, and so there is no upset from changes in the level of the head, no matter how quickly the giraffe moves.

Casual mothers

Mating and calving appear to take place all the year, with peak periods which may vary from one region to another. The gestation period is 420–468 days, the single calf being able to walk within an hour of birth, when it is 6 ft to the top of the head and weighs 117 lb. Reports vary about the suckling which is said to continue for 9 months, but in one study the calves were browsing at the age of one week and were not seen suckling after that. The bond between mother and infant is, in any case, a loose one. Giraffe milk has a high fat content and the young grow fast. Captive giraffes often live for over 20 years.

Defensive hoofs

Giraffes have few enemies. A lion may take a young calf or several lions may combine to kill an adult. Even these events are rare because the long legs and heavy hoofs can be used to deadly effect, striking down at an attacker.

Symbol of friendliness

Rock engravings of giraffes have been found over the whole of Africa and some of the most imposing are at Fezzan in the middle of what is now the Sahara desert. The animal must have lingered on in North Africa until 500 B.C. Some of the engravings are life size, or even larger, and many depict the trap used to capture giraffes, while others show typical features of its behaviour, including the necking. The engravings also show ostriches, dibatag, and gerenuk. Giraffes were also figured on the slate palettes, used for grinding malachite and haematite for eye-shadows, in Ancient Egypt, similar to that believed to portray the dibatag. The last giraffe depicted in Egyptian antiquities is on the tomb of Rameses the Great, 1225 BC.

There are references to the animal in Greek and Roman writings and a few pictures survive from the Roman era, but from then until the 7th or 8th century AD the principal records are in Arabic literature. The description given by Zakariya al-Qaswini in his 13th-century *Marvels of Creation* reflects the accepted view, that 'the giraffe is produced by the camel mare, the male hyaena and the wild cow'. The giraffe was taken to India by the Arabs, and from there to China, the first arriving in 1414 in the Imperial Zoological Garden in Peking. To the Chinese it symbolized gentleness and peace and the Arabs adopted this symbolism, so a gift of a giraffe became a sign of peace and friendliness between rulers.

In medieval Europe, and until the end of the 18th century, knowledge of the giraffe was based on descriptions in Greek and Roman writings and on hearsay accounts. It was at best a legendary beast.

class	**Mammalia**
order	**Artiodactyla**
family	**Giraffidae**
genus & species	***Giraffa camelopardalis***

Wiped out for its hide in many parts of its range, the present day distribution of the giraffe is much reduced. A number of races are recognised within the single species.

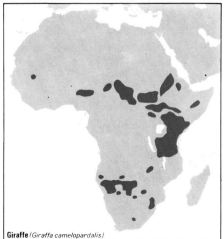

Giraffe *(Giraffa camelopardalis)*

One more . . .

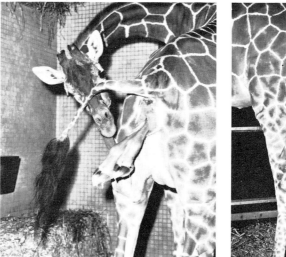
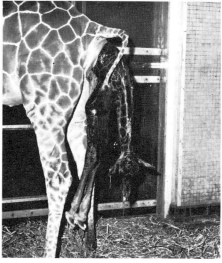

Below: The happy couple. A pair of giraffes circle one another in courtship ceremony.
Right: Casual birth. With a minimum of fuss, a calf is born in London Zoo—all 6 ft and 110 lb of it. After wobbling to its feet straight away, the calf can walk within an hour—very necessary in the wild, with many predators only too ready to snatch an easy meal.
Below right: First food. Although opinions differ about the time a giraffe calf spends suckling, it is known that the milk is highly nourishing, and the baby grows at an extraordinary rate.

Despite these happy domestic scenes, the relationship between mothers and calves is quite casual—they merely live in the same herd once weaning is over.

Giraffes at home

Far right: Using long tongue and mobile lips, a giraffe feeds on ground-growing plants.
Right: Top gear. A herd of females and young gallop away from a disturbance.
Below: Feathered grooms. A pair of oxpeckers feed on the parasites from the neck of a somewhat disgruntled giraffe.
Below right: The long way down. Giraffe at a waterhole during a drought in Nairobi Park. One might expect the blood to run into a giraffe's head in this awkward position, but a system of reservoirs and valves, inside the arteries, prevents this. A giraffe will drink regularly if there is water nearby, but in times of drought it can abstain for some time.
Below far right: Tough tongued eater. Ignoring thorns in its mouth, a giraffe makes the best of a sharp meal, while avoiding prickly branches with its flexible neck.

Okapia

N Myers: Bavaria

Phillipa Scott: Photo Res

Gene Wolfsheimer

*See-through skin and shining colours make glassfishes popular in aquaria. Left: Siamese glassfish **Chanda wolfii**. Above: **Chanda lala**.*

Glassfish

This is an obvious name for fishes that are transparent, with the skeleton and some internal organs clearly visible; yet although transparent they do not lack colour. A number of fishes are transparent or translucent but the name 'glassfish' is reserved for certain small fishes that are favourite aquarium fishes. In the same family, however, are large game or commercial fishes, including the snooks and the Nile perch. As we shall see, the glassfish and the Nile perch, although so different to look at, have one thing in common; they have both, at different times, ended in the ground.

The body is deep and strongly compressed from side-to-side. The dorsal fin is in two parts, that in front being supported by hard rays, the rear portion having one hard ray and up to 18 soft rays. The tailfin is either rounded or deeply forked.

The 8 or more species are found from East Africa through southern Asia to eastern Australia, the majority being in southeast Asia.

The 8 species of snooks live in the seas of tropical west and east Atlantic and the eastern Pacific. They readily enter rivers and may be 4½ ft long with a weight of 51 lb. The Nile perch, up to 7 ft long and more than 250 lb weight, is only one of several related African game species. It looks much more substantial than the glassfish and a special account of it will be given later.

Living gems for fertilizers

The Indian glassfish looks like a piece of crystal floating and reflecting colours in water. It is up to 3 in. long, greenish to yellowish but shining gold or iridescent bluish-green in reflected light. The flanks are marked with bars made up of tiny black dots, with a delicate violet stripe running from the gill-cover to the root of the tail. The fins are yellowish to rusty-red, the dorsal and anal fins with black rays and bordered with pale blue. Rays of paired fins are red or bluish.

It is the best known of the small glassfishes, and lives in fresh and brackish waters of India, Burma and Thailand. Its uneventful life is spent among water plants feeding on small aquatic animals such as insect larvae, crustaceans and worms. Its breeding habits are almost equally uneventful. In aquaria, according to Günther Sterba, spawning is triggered by morning sunshine raising the temperature, and a brief separation of the sexes, by putting them in separate tanks for a short time then reuniting them. The pair take up position side-by-side, quivering all the time. As the female lays the pair turn over to an upside-down position. The female lays her eggs among water plants to which they stick. She lays 4–6 at a time, repeating this until 200 or more have been laid. After this the parents take no further interest. The eggs hatch in 8–24 hours, depending on temperature, the baby fishes hanging from the water plants for 3–4 days after which they swim freely. Their food is small crustaceans, such as water fleas. The young glassfishes do not go in search of food but snap up any that drifts past them. It can be presumed that if food is scarce around the area at such times many

young fishes will die of starvation. Nevertheless, large numbers survive for, as William T Innes remarks in his *Exotic Aquarium Fishes*, this little gem treasured by aquarists is caught in large numbers in India and Burma for use as a fertilizer.

Family likenesses

Two people when related even distantly often share what we call a family likeness. In height, girth, colour of hair and in almost every way the two may be wholly unlike yet there is something that marks them as belonging to a family. It may be something very small, for example, a peculiarity in the way they walk, the shape of the lower lip, and so on. It is the same in classifying animals, and the family we are considering here is a fine example. Included in it are glassfishes, small, transparent, delicate; as well as snooks that are large, sturdy and not transparent and the 7ft robust giant, the Nile perch. From a casual glance they look most unlike yet each has a similar outline, and each has at least one small feature we call a family likeness. In each the lateral line, the line of sense-organs running along the flanks of fishes, goes right to the end of the tailfin, which is most unusual.

class	**Osteichthyes**
order	**Perciformes**
family	**Centropomidae**
genera & species	***Chanda ranga*** *Indian glassfish* ***Centropomus unidecimalis*** *snook others*

Leonard Lee Rue

Glass snake

Glass 'snakes' are, in fact, legless lizards that look like snakes. The Scheltopusik or Pallas' glass snake of southeast Europe and southwest Asia is nearly 4 ft long and about 2 in. across the body. It was first discovered by the naturalist Pallas on wooded slopes bordering the Volga. Since then it has been found as far west as Hungary and it is widespread throughout the Balkan peninsula. Another living in northeast India and Burma is 15 in. long and the glass snake of southern China is 2 ft long. There is another glass snake in Morocco and 3 others in North America, up to 3 ft long, ranging from Lake Michigan southwards through the eastern and southern states and into Mexico. One American species **O. ventralis** *is brown, olive or black with green spots or stripes and greenish-white underneath.*

Two-thirds of their length is made up of tail, whereas in snakes the tail makes up only a small fraction of the total length. Pallas' glass snake is bronze, yellow or chestnut-brown, often with tiny pale spots, and very old individuals are coppery-red. The glass snake of southern China has an olive back and bright blue flanks. All glass snakes have a deep furrow running along each side of the body from the neck to the vent. There is no trace of the forelimbs and, in the European and North African species, there is a barely noticeable stump of a hindlimb at the rear end of the furrow.

Snake-like but not snakes

Glass snakes live in fields or copses, among heaps of stones or in bare rocky places. They avoid dense woods. They are not as agile as snakes but they can clamber over rocks easily. They do not climb trees, and they avoid water. Their habit is to hide under fallen leaves or burrow just beneath the surface where the soil is sandy and light. When they do come out they move over the ground like snakes but with a less graceful action. When chased they move with a rapid twisting of the body, stopping every 2–3 yd for a rest.

Glass snakes feed by day on insects, especially grasshoppers. They sometimes take mice, lizards, fledgling birds and the eggs of snakes and birds. Live prey is twisted rapidly round and round or beaten against the ground until stunned and then chewed with powerful jaws and swallowed whole. Glass snakes are said to eat snakes, including adders. When eating an egg they crack the shell with their jaws and ladle out the con-

tents with their flat forked tongues. The American glass snake, also called glass-lizard or joint snake, seems to spend more time burrowing than the European form. It has a similar diet but is said to eat earthworms as well as other underground animals.

The females lay their inch-long eggs under moss or dead leaves, 8–10 at a time. They take about a month to hatch, the female guarding them during that time in a half-hearted way. The newly-hatched glass snake is 5 in. long, ashen-grey with dark spots and bands along the back and dark vertical stripes on the sides of the head. They take several years to reach maturity and the glass snakes are said to live up to 60 years.

Two lines of defence

Little is known about the enemies of glass snakes. They would be likely to be taken by large birds of prey. They have, however, two lines of defence. Like other lizards they can shed their tails when attacked, and if held in the hand they twine round it in a most unpleasant manner, which would probably deter all but a large or a persistent predator.

Falling to bits

Glass snakes are named for their reputation of breaking into pieces when struck with a stick. The legend continues that the pieces

later reassemble and that the lizard is none the worse for its adventure. As in other lizards the tail is shed in moments of alarm, but in glass snakes it also breaks into several pieces. Because the tail is so long, the body of a glass snake that has just cast its tail looks very small, little bigger than one of the portions of the shed tail, so it looks as if the whole animal is in pieces.

class	**Reptilia**
order	**Squamata**
suborder	**Sauria**
family	**Anguidae**
genus & species	***Ophisaurus apodus*** *European glass snake* ***O. ventralis*** *N. American glass snake* *others*

△ *Brittle-tailed reptile: the 'glass' half of this animal's name is perhaps justified by the way its tail will fall off and break into several pieces in moments of alarm. 'Snake', however, does not apply; it is a legless lizard.*
▷ *Twisting sprinter—a European glass snake. Glass snakes do not move with the wriggling expertise of true snakes, especially when frightened; they use a twisting movement and have to stop for a rest every 2−3 yd.*

Walter Jarchow

1043

Gliding frog

There are a few species of frogs which are also referred to as 'the so-called flying frogs', or else they are called 'flying' frogs. The writer then goes on to say that of course they do not fly, they only glide. It is high time, therefore, that we stopped calling them flying frogs and followed the lead given, for example, by Doris B Cochran, of the United States National Museum, and called them gliding frogs, which is what they are.

The gliding frogs are members of a family of tree frogs, Rhacophoridae, which will be dealt with later. The most common are the Malayan and Wallace's gliding frogs which are 4 in. long in the head and body, shining green above, yellow on flanks and white underneath. They range from Malaya to Borneo. As with other tree frogs of this family the ends of the toes on all four feet have sucker discs at the tips, for clinging to trees. Gliding frogs differ in having the toes of all four feet longer than usual and fully webbed.

Jumping and gliding

Gliding frogs spend the day in trees and tall bushes holding on by the discs on their toes. In strong sunlight they are a greenish-blue, turning to green in the evening and finally to black, the change taking place more rapidly in the males than the females. They become active at night, leaping from branch to branch and taking gliding leaps from tree to tree. The leaps may be up to 6 ft but the glide may cover 40–50 ft to the base of the next tree. In a glide the toes are fully stretched and held rigid and the underside of the body is drawn up, giving a concave surface that increases the lift. The direction and length of a glide can be controlled to some extent.

Foam nests

Gliding frogs feed mainly on grasshoppers but take other insects as well and when breeding they do not take to water but make foam nests among large leaves. While mating the male clings on the female's back, as is usual in frogs. As the eggs are laid quantities of albumen are given out with them and both female and male beat this into a frothy mass with a paddling action of the hindlegs. The outside of the mass hardens while the inside of it becomes more and more fluid. The eggs float in this until rain washes either the eggs, or the tadpoles, out of the nest, to fall into pools below. If no rain falls the outer crust eventually liquefies to release eggs or tadpoles.

Frogs' flying school

The first Europeans to learn about these frogs heard the story from Chinese labourers in southeast Asia who spoke of the frogs flying down from the trees. The story that there were frogs that flew was accepted at first. Then came disbelief and this was reinforced by a curious accident. Alfred Russel Wallace, the distinguished naturalist, who

worked so much in the southeast Asian region, calculated that the area of the spread feet with their webs was sufficient to enable the frogs to glide. He made an error in his calculations and when this was detected the story of flying frogs became further discredited. Few zoologists had ever seen the gliding frog alive so it was difficult to check Wallace's statement or those of the Chinese in Malaya. In 1926, however, HB Cott carried out experiments with the Brazilian tree frog *Hyla venulosa* which showed that even tree frogs with less webbing than gliding frogs could fall from considerable heights and land safely on their feet. He dropped the frogs from a tower 140 ft high and the frogs landed on the ground 90 ft out from the base of the tower. They reached the ground at such a slow speed that they were quite unhurt. Almost any small tree-living animal will do

the same and the reason is that they spread their legs and keep their body the right way up, as a cat does when it falls from a height, and this acts as a brake. By contrast, the ordinary common frog, although the webs on its feet are larger than those of a tree frog, simply tumbles head over heels when it falls and plummets straight down. It only needs that little extra webbing on the feet, which gliding frogs have, to keep them gliding.

class	**Amphibia**
order	**Salientia**
family	**Rhacophoridae**
genus & species	***Rhacophorus nigropalmatus*** Wallace's gliding frog ***R. reinwardtii*** Malayan gliding frog

▽ *Ready to go: a Siamese gliding frog* **Rhacophorus prominanus** *takes aim for the leap which will start its long glide towards the base of the next tree—perhaps 50 ft away.*

Lim Boo Liat

▽ *Airborne amphibian: Bornean gliding frog on the way down, each webbed foot a tiny parachute. Even the body is held concave to add to the gliding surface and so increase lift.*

D Davis

Glowworm

The glowworm is a beetle belonging to the family Lampyridae which also includes the fireflies (p. 912). Centuries ago anything that was long and crawling was called a worm. The female glowworm lacks wings and it was this and her general appearance that was responsible for the name.

Male and female of the common English glowworm **Lampyris noctiluca** are yellowish grey-brown. The male has large eyes and two very tiny light-producing organs at the tip of the abdomen. He also has wings covered by the usual wing cases of beetles, and his length is about ½ in. The female, slightly longer than the male, differs little in shape from the larva and the last three segments of the body, on the underside, are yellowish and strongly luminescent.

A second species of glowworm **Phosphaenus hemipterus** has been found but rarely in parts of southern England. It is, however, widespread over continental Europe.

The lure of the lights

Adult glowworms are most active in June and July. Preferring slightly damp places, they may be found on hedgerow banks, hillsides and in rough meadows, especially where there is a plentiful supply of snails. By day they hide in cracks and crevices. After nightfall the female climbs onto a prominent piece of foliage and takes up a position head down so her luminous end is prominently displayed. Her method of light-production is the same as in the firefly (see p. 912). Beneath the light-producing bands is a whitish, opaque layer which not only prevents absorption of the light into the body, but reflects it back, making full use of all the light. The winged male homes on the female's light for mating. The light may be visible to us over 100 yd or so under suitable conditions, but may be 'doused' as we approach and switched on again after an interval. By contrast, the larvae light up as a result of being disturbed, which suggests that in them the luminescence may serve as a defence, frightening away some enemies. The larvae's light also is slightly different from that of the adults, being more intensely green.

Short-lived adults

The pale yellow eggs are 1 mm diameter. Usually they are laid in ones and twos over a period of a couple of days on grass stems or moss, or in or on the soil. They hatch in a fortnight, the larvae being almost exact miniatures of the adult females except for the simpler structure of the legs and a series of paler spots at the front corners of each body segment. Growing by a series of moults, the larvae reach the adult stage in three years. The pupa of the male differs from that of the female, reflecting the different appearance of the adults. Emerging from the pupae after about 8 or 9 days, usually in April or May, the adults live for only a short while after mating and egg-laying. During mating neither sex glows.

John Markham

△ Fickle flasher: having attracted three males to her powerful light, a female glowworm mates with one, ignored by her disappointed suitors.

▽ Incandescent cousin: female African beetle of the closely related family Phengodidae waiting in the grass for response to her light.

Anthony Bannister: NHPA

Larvae feed, parents starve

Adult glowworms take no food, although it is often asserted that they do. The larvae feed on snails which they discover by following their slime trails. They drive their hollow, curved mandibles into the mollusc and inject a dark fluid, partly paralysing and partly digestive. This rapidly reduces the snail's tissues to a pre-digested soup-like liquid which the glowworm then sucks up. Newly-hatched glowworms are only $\frac{1}{5}$ in. long. They feed on the smaller snails. Sometimes the larvae feed communally, crowding round the lip of the shell and feeding side by side. After a meal the glowworm pushes out a white sponge-like device from its anus. With this it can clean away from its head and back any remains of slime resulting from its meal.

Lucky to survive

Glowworms fall victim to any insect-eating animal, despite the glowing lights on their bodies, but especially to toads and hedgehogs, both of which feed at night. Some are eaten by frogs and spiders, and there are mites which penetrate the soft joints between the body segments of the larvae and feed on their body fluids. The larvae are particularly vulnerable to mites when they have shed their skins at the periodic moults, making them fair game for these parasites.

On the decline

The twinkling lights of a modern city are an irresistible attraction to the eye of young and old alike. It is doubtful, however, whether any of the artificial illumination produced by man has the same aesthetic quality as that from a well-stocked colony of glowworms seen on a moonless night. It is not surprising that poets have made so much of this. Unfortunately, the chances of seeing it today, at least in Britain, are much smaller than in times past. Glowworms, useful and attractive insects, have died out from many areas where they were once common. The reasons for this are not easy to see, but it almost certainly springs from the pressure on land for housing, factories, intensive farming, combined with more efficient draining of the land. No doubt the use of insecticides is also partly to blame. What is quite certain is that it is not natural enemies that have brought about his fall in numbers, because toads and hedgehogs are all less numerous than they used to be.

Ironically, there may be another reason. Many insects are irresistibly attracted to artificial light, and in this the male glowworm is no exception, in spite of the fact that it has its own, highly individual 'bright light' to go to—that emitted by the female. Even the weak, flickering light of a candle-flame will attract a glowworm, as Gilbert White, father of field naturalists, records. In many areas, it seems, modern artificial lighting systems have become a serious threat to glowworm survival, in that the male glowworms are finding them far more alluring than the more modest glow produced by the females, which as a result may languish in vain and even die 'old maids'! Once attracted to the lights of large buildings the male insects may damage themselves in hitting or being burnt by them, and then fall to the ground stunned or dazzled, to be subsequently eaten by a variety of small animals; or the attraction may simply disrupt the delicate balance of nocturnal flight activity. Fortunately there are still many areas in England where such hazards are less pronounced, as is indicated by the fact that the greatest numbers of glowworms are found in areas which are comparatively less developed industrially.

phylum	**Arthropoda**
class	**Insecta**
order	**Coleoptera**
family	**Lampyridae**
genus & species	***Lampyris noctiluca***

Making the most of youth: doomed to starvation as an adult, a glowworm larva gorges itself on a tiny garden snail (12 × life size).

GS Giacomenii

Gnu

Often known by their Afrikaans name, wildebeest, gnus are ugly cow-like antelopes, up to 4 ft at the shoulder, with short thick necks and large heads with a tuft of long hair on the muzzle, a throat fringe and a mane. The males weigh up to 460 lb, the females up to 360 lb. There are two species, the white-tailed gnu, or black wildebeest, and the brindled gnu, or blue wildebeest. The former, extinct

Following the young grass

The white-bearded race of the brindled gnu was studied in 1963 by Lee and Martha Talbot in West Masailand (centred on the Serengeti plains), where they counted 239 516 of them. The animals move about freely; in the wet season they are scattered over the plains, and in the dry season they move through the surrounding bush, along streams, seeking new grass produced by local showers. In the dry season the movements between these limited areas of new grass lead to massing, and huge numbers are to be seen in one place. It is not a true,

calves are well developed, and can follow their mothers within 4–5 minutes of birth. There is, however, a heavy loss through predation and through calves becoming separated from their mothers. Within a few weeks almost half the season's crop of calves are dead. When the surviving calves are 6–7 months old, a rinderpest epidemic further decimates them, and this lasts until 11–12 months after birth. This is known as 'yearling disease'. It arises at this time due to the loss of the initial colostral immunity, but does not bother adults. The colostral immunity is imparted by the

△ *Dawn patrol: Gnus trek in the cool of morning, seeking new grass before the intense midday heat forces them to rest in shade.*

in the wild but preserved on private land in South Africa, has a long-haired white tail and forward-curving horns. The latter, slightly larger, has an equally horselike black tail and laterally curved horns; instead of being blackish like the other, the brindled gnu is grey with brownish bands on neck, shoulders and the front part of each flank. The long tail is used to make fly-whisks, which are a symbol of rank in East and South Africa. The white-tailed gnu has always been restricted to South Africa. The brindled gnu occurs in both South and East Africa, and is still abundant.

regular migration, however, although the animals may move as much as 30 miles in a day. The gnu feed in the morning and evening, seeking shade in the heat of the day. They are sheep-like in that they tend to follow anything moving in a determined manner—other gnu, other animals, even Land Rovers. Several species of grass are eaten, but only the fresh young growth, when the sprouts are not more than 4 in. high. Where the grass is regularly burned, this helps the gnu.

Democratic love-making

The rut is in April and May. The peak of calving comes 9 months later, in January and February, when the plains are green. The

mother to the calf in the first flow of her milk. This milk is called the colostrum and contains proteins, which pass directly through the baby's stomach wall into the bloodstream. These proteins include some of the mother's antibodies, which temporarily protect the infant from disease. The severity of yearling disease depends on the density of population, but taking everything into account there is an average loss of 80% of the calves each year. The 20% left form 8% of the population. Since the numbers of gnu remain steady from year to year this means that 8% of adults are lost each year.

The calf stays with its mother until the next one is born, after which the cow prevents the elder calf from suckling. Bull

The white-tailed gnu, with elegantly forward-curving horns, is extinct in the wild.

Klaus Paysan

beest; since there are about 700 lions there the yearly kill per lion is about 16. In the Talbots' study, 91·1% of the predation was by lions, 3·3% by cheetah, 2·2% leopard, 2·2% hyaena, 1·1% wild dog. The toll due to hunting (poaching) and accidents is about twice as important as that due to predators other than the lion. Gnu do not defend themselves against lions, but against cheetahs and wild dogs they have been known to form a circle, like musk oxen.

Sharing out the food

The ecology of the hoofed animals on the Serengeti provides a striking lesson in natural land-use. The gnu feed only on young shoots, as we have seen. Zebra feed on the same grasses but at a later stage of growth. Topi feed on the same species but on old grass. Yet other species feed on different grasses growing in the same places. Thus the Serengeti can support a far greater quantity of wild hoofed animals than it could domestic cattle, and is potentially much more valuable as a source of protein.

The enormous wastage of calves in their first year gives great scope to natural selection and comes as a surprise to those accustomed to thinking of large hoofed animals as slow breeders and consequently slow in evolving. Several races of brindled gnu exist. This is because to support gnus a habitat must provide new grass all the year round. Such places are not common, so the gnus tend to be in areas isolated from each other. This gives rise to differences between the groups, just as animals on groups of islands develop into different species (see Darwin's finches, p. 751). On the Serengeti, they are second in abundance only to Thomson's gazelle, of which there are between 5 and 8 million there. And there are twice as many gnu as there are zebra. On plains, south of Nairobi, gnu were almost wiped out by hunting but they have recovered rapidly. There are now some 9 000 there.

class	**Mammalia**
order	**Artiodactyla**
family	**Bovidae**
genus	***Connochaetes gnou***
& species	*white-tailed gnu*
	C. taurinus *brindled gnu*

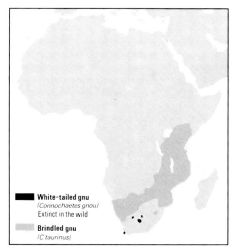

White-tailed gnu
(Connochaetes gnou)
Extinct in the wild

Brindled gnu
(C taurinus)

yearlings now form separate herds, while the young cows remain in the cows' herd.

The rut takes place during the dry season. When the moving herds halt awhile where food is abundant, some of the males establish harems, which may contain as few as 2–3 females or as many as 150 females and young. Each male herds his harem tightly, running round and round it. Often as many as three bulls herd the same harem. They are not aggressive towards one another, and they have no hierarchy. A bull herding runs with a rocking gait, head held high. The females, the young and the non-active bulls keep the normal head-down position. The harem forms the centre of a territory established for the time being by one or several bulls. If a male approaches in rut position from the neighbouring herd, the bulls of the threatened herd go to meet him. The nearest one rushes forward, the rivals drop to their knees, butt and spar, get up, snort, look round, then retire or do it again. The breeding herds are stable for several days until the food is gone and the gnus must move on. Then the males retire to the margins of the migrating herd either

singly or in small groups. Each time there is a pause in the mass movement, the males round up harems, and merge back into the mass when it begins to move again. Only a small proportion of bulls form harems each time, so different individuals are active at each stop. Non-active bulls can feed close to the breeding herds without being attacked. In fact, if they graze too close, they may be rounded up by other males like cows and calves! Some males establish a territory first, and then try to drive females into it. Some old males do not even migrate, but establish home ranges near water.

Gnus may live 20 years. Each year 83% of yearling cows breed; and 95% of the rest. At birth there are 170 males to 100 females; after a year the ratio is 117:100, and after 1½ the adult ratio of 108:100 is reached.

Lions most feared

Far and away the most important predator of the gnu is the lion. The 8% turnover of the population each year represents 18 000 animals, and these are almost entirely accounted for by lions. At least half of the lion's prey on the Serengeti consists of wilde-

Goats browsing in semi-desert. When presented with more lush conditions they will soon eat and spoil them until the land is like this.

Goat

Scientifically, it is not easy to sort sheep from goats. The distinguishing features are that the horns of sheep grow to the sides of the head, those of goats curve upwards and backwards and are worn by both sexes. Male goats have a strong smell and wear beards. In goats the forehead is convex, not concave as in sheep.

There are five species of wild goat, including the ibexes and the markhor. The wild goat **Capra hircus** *from which the domesticated goat was derived, ranges from southeast Europe through Asia Minor to Persia and Pakistan. Domestication can be traced to 6–7 thousand years ago and it may have been earlier.*

Goats are 4½ ft long in body and head, the tail is 6 in., they are 3 ft high at the shoulders and weigh up to 260 lb, the males being larger than the females. The horns of males are sweeping and scimitar shaped, up to

52 in. long, compressed sideways and ornamented along the inner front edge with large knobs. The horns of the females are shorter and more slender. The coat is typically reddish-brown in summer, greyish-brown in winter with black markings on the body and limbs.

Desert-making goats

Goats usually live in rugged, rocky or mountainous country, but sometimes on lowland plains. Where hunted they become extremely wary, and difficult to stalk, as their sure-footed skill as they progress from rock to rock is legendary. They generally move about in herds of 5–20, led by an old female. When living on mountains they may go up almost to the snow-line but in winter migrate down to lower levels, returning in spring to the fresh pastures. Goats do not sleep; they merely have periods of drowsiness.

Goats will eat straw, and have been seen to scratch their backs with straws held in the mouth. Like sheep, goats chew the cud,

but whereas sheep take mainly grass, goats browse chiefly on leaves and twigs as well. They will eat desert scrub and climb into trees to browse, and goats have been seen to jump onto the backs of donkeys to reach the lower boughs, and from there move to higher and higher boughs by jumps. They readily take bark, will eat paper and are notorious for eating linen cloth. In this they are helped by protozoa living in the gut which pre-digest cellulose. Domestic goats will eat the foliage of yew, which may be fatal to horses and cattle, and suffer only a temporary diarrhoea. Released on oceanic islands, goats have reduced earthly paradises to barren soil with only low vegetation. In the Near and Middle East herds of goats have contributed to the formation of deserts.

Climbers from birth

A female goat over two years old is known as a nanny-goat, the male is a buck or billy-goat. Both are relatively recent names, the first having been used since 1788, the second since 1861. Mating is normally in autumn and the kids, born 147–180 days later, are able to run shortly after birth and soon

Soyka Anthony

△ *A magnificent face in the crowd; even this buck with sweeping scimitar horns obeys the old nanny-goat who leads the herd.*

◁ *Adept climbers from birth—A goat has even been known to jump on a donkey's back to reach the boughs of an appetising tree.*

△▷ *Out on a limb; but the sure-footed agility displayed by these youngsters merely extends the area goats can devastate.*

▷ *Every kid needs its mum now and then, especially if he is the only one as a goat is likely to be.*

▽ *Domesticated 7 000 years ago, the goat has lived alongside man and provided him with milk and meat. But even a small herd left to run wild will multiply at an embarrassing rate and soon convert an island paradise into the barren hillside which is its natural habitat.*

Mondadoripress

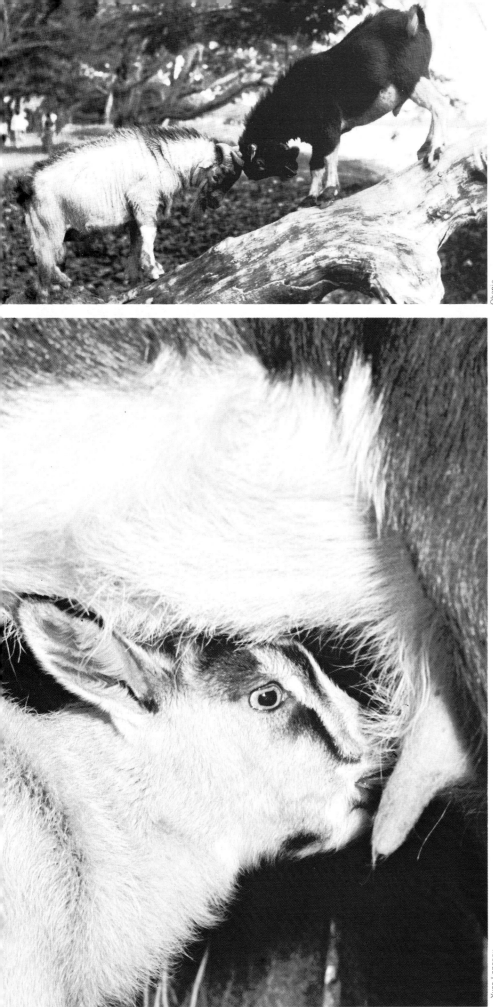

become adept at climbing. There are one, sometimes two at a birth, exceptionally three or four. Sexual maturity is reached in about 12 months, when the male is known as a buckling, the female as a goatling. The life span is up to 18 years.

Indestructible spoilers

Goats have probably always been more useful for their milk than for their hair or flesh. Their flesh is somewhat rank and the hair short, but sometimes used for spinning, especially from longhaired breeds such as the Angora and the Kashmir. In the days of sail, ships took goats on board to provide fresh milk as well as meat. Ships' captains would put goats ashore on oceanic islands for the use of castaways, or to get rid of surplus. The marooned goats multiplied and, as on St Helena and other islands, denuded the flora. In 1773 Captain James Cook put goats ashore in New Zealand. These went wild and multiplied. Later goats were taken there for other purposes, to feed those building roads and railways, for use in miners' camps, and also to prevent introduced bramble, gorse and bracken running amok.

In fact, the goats barked trees, ate shrubs, brought many native plants to the verge of extinction and cleared the ground of mosses that not only held water but protected the topsoil from wind erosion. Their hoofs cut the turf so that it was washed away by rain, so adding to the erosion. The natural home of a goat is the barren hillside and wherever goats go they convert the landscape into their natural habitat.

The speed at which goats multiply is also an embarrassment. In 1698 an English ship put into the harbour of Bonavista. Two Negroes went aboard and offered the captain all the goats he cared to take away. There were only 12 people living on the island and not only were the goats eating everything but they were so tame nobody could go anywhere without a crowd of goats following.

Holinshed, in his *Chronicles of England,* 1577, wrote: 'Goats we have in plenty, and of sundry colours, in the west parts of England; especially in and towards Wales, and among the rocky hills, by whom the owners do reap no small advantage.' What the advantage was he did not say but it is believed that goats were deliberately allowed to go wild in these regions by the sheep farmers. In the Welsh mountains grass grows lush in inaccessible places. Sheep attracted up by the grass cannot get down and have to be retrieved. Wild goats, better climbers than the sheep, climb the high rocks and eat the grass (so removing temptation for the sheep) and have no difficulty in descending.

class	**Mammalia**
order	**Artiodactyla**
family	**Bovidae**
genus & species	***Capra hircus***

1051

The humble goatfish, once worth its weight in silver at a Roman banquet, where it was brought alive to the table in a glass bowl.

Goatfish

The red mullet or surmullet is the member of the family Mullidae best known in Britain, but as most of the 42 species have been called goatfishes the name is used here. The true mullets belong to the family Mugilidae and are only distantly related. Goatfishes are long-bodied with two short dorsal fins, the one in front being spiny, the other soft. Their chief feature is a pair of long barbels under the chin, fancifully likened to a goat's beard. The barbels are flexible and can be swung forward or brought back to lie under the throat, where they are barely visible. The majority of goatfishes are under 10 in. long but a few species reach 2 ft.

Goatfishes live mainly in tropical waters but some are found in temperate seas. The red mullet is tropical and subtropical but ranges as far north as Norway. It is abundant in the Mediterranean. The spotted goatfish of the Bahamas and Atlantic seaboard of North America is mottled red. All goatfishes are red, orange or golden. The red mullet, for example, may be all red or it may be red on the back

and sides with 3—5 longitudinal bright yellow stripes along the flanks. All goatfishes are noted for their rapid colour changes, not only while alive but also when dying.

Touch and taste in one

Typical goatfishes live inshore, in shallow waters and around coral reefs. Some are solitary, others live in shoals. They feed on worms, molluscs and crustaceans like shrimps. As they swim over the seabed they use their barbels as fingers, moving them actively to search the sand for food. As well as organs of touch the barbels are organs of taste, each bearing many taste-buds.

Spawning is in June and July, in the red mullet, and as in all goatfishes the eggs float at the surface. They are about $\frac{1}{30}$ in. diameter and hatch in 3—4 days. At first the baby fishes have a large yolk sac which projects well forward beyond the tip of the head.

Technicolor death

The colours of a goatfish, like those of the dolphin fish (p. 788) are brightest at the moment of capture and fade when the fish is dead. In Roman times, when the red mullet was, as it is now, a valuable food-fish, it was brought alive to the banqueting

table in a glass bowl. The guests were able to watch it swimming round and round and then enjoy the spectacular display of colour changes as it died. From tints of brightest scarlet the fish would flash to greenish red against streaks of ash-grey. Such was their popularity that red mullet were kept in special ponds and at least one wealthy Roman was reportedly more concerned with the welfare of his mullet than of his slaves. Each fish was worth its weight in silver, and was the equivalent of one slave in value.

Inevitably there arose a legend, but not about the colour. Michel de Montaigne, 16th-century French essayist, claimed that when the mullet was hooked a companion would swim across the line just above the hook, trying to cut it with the saw edge formed by the spiny dorsal fin.

class	**Osteichthyes**
order	**Perciformes**
family	**Mullidae**
genera & species	*Mullus surmuletus* red mullet *Parupeneus multifasciatus* common goatfish *Pseudupeneus maculatus* spotted goatfish, others

Fingers with taste buds: goatfish barbels.

Goat moth

The goat moth is so called on account of the strong and unpleasant smell of its larva, which burrows in the wood of trees. It is a large, stout insect with brown intricately mottled wings spanning 3 in. or more and is one of three British species belonging to the family Cossidae. These are regarded as primitive moths related to the family of small or minute moths called the Tortricidae. They are also called carpenter moths.

Don't take it home

The goat moth flies at night and is attracted to light. By day it sits on the trunks and branches of trees, where its colour and markings give it very effective camouflage. The larva burrows in the living wood, especially of willows and poplars. It is over 3 in. long when fully grown and stout in proportion, and its burrowing severely damages the timber of the tree in which it feeds. Affected trees exude a dark fluid from the openings of the burrows and this has a powerful smell, somewhat like that of a male goat. In spite of its unpleasant smell, other butterflies and moths are strongly attracted to the fluid, and an infested tree is worth keeping under observation by day and night.

The caterpillar is fully grown sometime in spring or summer, and often comes out of the tree in which it has lived and fed, to wander about seeking a place to pupate. This is the stage at which it is most often seen, the huge chestnut- and flesh-coloured larva being very conspicuous. If such a larva is taken home and put in a tin with some pieces of decayed wood it will spin a cocoon and pupate. It is useless to confine a goat moth larva in a wooden box as it will eat its way out in a very short time, and probably not all members of the household will be happy to encounter it in its subsequent wanderings.

The other two British moths of the family Cossidae are the leopard moth, whose larva also feeds in trees, and the reed leopard. The latter is rather rare, confined to fens and marshes, and its larva lives in the stems of reeds. The larva of the leopard moth lives in the trunks and branches of various trees, including fruit trees, where it may do some damage. It has been introduced into the United States, no doubt in timber imported from Europe, and is a considerable pest in trees in city parks. Both these moths are also found in Japan, and the reed leopard is found in China.

In the tropics and subtropics, especially those of Australia, some very large relatives of the goat moth are found. One *Xyleutes boisduvali* has a wing span of up to 10 in. and a body that has been described as resembling a small banana in shape and size.

Three-year larva

The eggs are laid on the bark of a tree and the larvae on hatching burrow under the bark and feed there for a year or so, eating their way into the solid wood as they grow larger. In the wild state they take up to three years to complete their growth.

Young goat moth larva (6 × life size).

Recipe for quick growth

The proboscis of the adult moth is vestigial and it must be supposed that the insect does not feed at all. Rather curiously, however, there are records of it visiting the bait of treacle painted on to tree trunks by moth collectors.

The larva eats wood throughout its long life and must consume great quantities of it. It is a matter of interest that if young goat moth larvae are fed on beetroot they complete their growth and come to full size in only a year.

Goat moths in history

The caterpillar of the goat moth has always attracted attention. In the 1750s a French entomologist, P Lyonnet, made a most detailed study of this larva and published a book about it. Among the facts he established were that, from the time of hatching from the egg to full growth, it increases its weight 72 000 times. Also in the course of dissecting it he discovered 4 061 muscles in its body. A second book, describing the pupa and the moth, was published after the author's death.

The Roman writer Pliny, who lived in the first century AD, wrote a monumental Natural History in 37 volumes, and one

Poplar riddled by grown larvae.

of the items he describes is a sort of large 'worm' that lived in the wood of oak trees and was highly esteemed as a luxury by gourmets of the time. The goat moth larva does sometimes live in oaks, and it has generally been assumed that this is what Pliny's edible wood-boring worms were, though there is no detailed description of them to serve as proof of this. If the ancient Romans did really eat these huge smelly caterpillars they must have had remarkably robust appetites.

phylum	**Arthropoda**
class	**Insecta**
order	**Lepidoptera**
family	**Cossidae**
genus & species	***Cossus cossus***

Adult goat moth. The larvae of this drab insect increase their weight 72 000 times to become fat and 3 in. long. Their voracious appetite damages poplars and willows, but their greed was repaid in kind many years ago; despite their goat-like smell, the Romans considered these repulsive larvae a delicacy, if the writer Pliny is to be believed.

Goby

*Gobies are the Lilliputians of the fish world, most gobies being under 3 in. long and many not much more than 1 in. long. The giant goby **Gobius cobitis** of the Mediterranean and western Europe does not exceed 9 in. and is usually 4—5 in. Most of them have little commercial value and so tend to be overlooked. Some of the largest among the nearly 500 species in the family are the mudskippers, which will be covered under that name. Other large gobies are the guavina **Gobiomorus dormitor** of Central America, 2 ft long, and the several species of **Bunaka** of the Indo-Australian region, of nearly the same size, which are valuable food-fishes. The smallest is the Luzon goby **Pandaka pygmaea** of the streams and lakes of the Philippines, barely ½ in. long, the smallest vertebrate.*

Mainly marine, but with many species entering brackish estuaries, gobies are colourful fishes with flattened heads, large eyes and short snouts. The eyes are high up on the head, often almost touching each other. There are two dorsal fins and the margins of the pelvic fins are joined to form a sucker.

Holing up for safety

As they are small it is natural that gobies should live in places where safe retreats are near at hand. Usually each fish has its own retreat from which it sallies forth to feed and to which it returns. The habitat is variable. Many gobies are bottom living, especially on rocky shores, some being left behind as the tide ebbs and sheltering under stones in rock pools. Others live in burrows in sand or mud, or shelter among branching corals. Some gobies have been elusive, regarded as rare for years, and then turning up unexpectedly in large numbers in a bay or a fiord. Since biologists began skin-diving, so-called rare species have been found to be common. The Catalina or blue-banded goby, for example, was first found in 1890. Few specimens were seen then or later until 1938 when an early skin-diving biologist found it was common, living in crevices in the rocks. New species have been discovered which could not have been otherwise brought to light because they live among rocky reefs, spending much of their time in crevices, where nets cannot reach them. A few gobies live among seaweeds in shallow inshore waters, and fewer still live in shoals in open water. Wherever they live their food is small invertebrates, especially the small crustaceans, and they also eat any small items of dead flesh that come to rest on the seabed.

Model fathers

By contrast with their retiring nature at other times the male gobies are aggressive towards each other during the breeding season. This is a matter of fighting over territories, in this case an area of rock, coral or other surface where the female will lay her eggs. After pairing, the male goby

Jane Burton : Photo Res

acts as guardian to the female while she is laying her eggs. Each egg is oval or pear-shaped, about $\frac{1}{16}$ in. long, and usually has a short stalk, the clump of eggs being fastened to a solid surface as they are laid. The 'nest' may be on rock or coral or in an empty shell. Having laid her clutch of about 100 eggs the female departs, leaving the male to guard it for anything up to a fortnight. He aerates the eggs by fanning them with his fins. The newly-hatched gobies are well developed and soon grow to look like their parents. Douglas Wilson has watched the sand goby *Pomatoschistus minutus* guarding eggs in an empty mollusc shell. If a shrimp or baby flatfish comes near he drives it off. When the shell with its eggs is removed for a few moments he swims back and forth over the spot in what seems a frenzied manner, and when the shell is put back he fusses over it like any conscientious mother to restore it to its original position, carrying tiny stones away with his mouth until the shell and the eggs are in order again.

Fried fish fry
Gobies are eaten by the usual predatory fishes, as well as diving seabirds such as divers, but little more is known of their enemies. Gobies are sometimes accidentally included in whitebait but apart from the few larger species taken for food in the Far East the only important fishery is in the northern Philippines. There a freshwater goby spawns in the sea and its $\frac{1}{2}$in. fry return in huge shoals to the mouths of the rivers. From September to March these are netted in the streams and rivers and sold under the name *ipon*, which is fried in oil or made into a paste called *bagoong*.

Unlikely partnerships
Gobies of the genus *Parioglossus* depart from the usual habit of keeping near their hiding places and 'hover' in mid-water in shoals of thousands. When disturbed they dive into the nearest coral heads. Related species of *Vireosa* do much the same except that they dive into the gaping shells of oysters and giant clams. Their entry alarms the molluscs which close their shells, so giving the gobies added security.

The habit of sheltering in cracks, crevices and burrows has led to several instances of commensalism (living together). The arrow goby *Clevelandia ios* of California shares

Leopard-spotted goby **Thorogobius ephippiatus** *in its shelter (fan worm* **Bispira volutacornis** *in foreground).*

DP Wilson

holes in mud-flats with a pea crab and a burrowing worm. The goby will carry large pieces of food, too big for it to swallow, for the crab to tear apart, then wait and pick up the crumbs. The blind goby *Typhlogobius californiensis*, also of California, lives in holes dug by the ghost shrimp. Should the shrimp die its goby companion is doomed unless it can find an unattached shrimp to live with. Several species of *Smilogobius* around the coasts of the Indo-Pacific region team up with snapping shrimps which dig and maintain the burrow, constantly shovelling away the loose sand, while the goby maintains a watch near its mouth. At the slightest alarm the goby dives into the burrow and the shrimp follows. The fish is the first to leave when things have settled down, and the shrimp then comes out to resume digging. It is a perfect partnership except that the goby is apt to feed on the shrimp's babies. A less damaging relationship is found between the neon goby *Elacatinus oceanops* and several species of larger fishes; it cleans parasites from them.

Looking before leaping
When dealing with genets (p. 1011) the suggestion was made that nocturnal animals carry in their memory a knowledge of their surroundings. Something of the same sort has been worked out for a goby *Bathygobius soporator*. This lives in pools when the tide is out and can find its way down the beach to the sea, if need be, by jumping from one pool to another. It is unable to see the next pool at the moment it takes off yet can leap with precision and not get stranded on dry land in between. This was carefully studied and the remarkable conclusion was reached that as the fish swims above the seabed at high tide it learns the topography of it so thoroughly that when the tide is out it knows the layout of the pools from high up the beach to the water's edge.

class	Osteichthyes
order	Perciformes
family	Gobiidae

◁ *Rock goby showing sucker of pelvic fins.*

▽ *Rock goby* **Gobius paganellus** *is a model father who cherishes the eggs until they hatch.*

Heather Angel

Godwit

Godwits are large waders related to snipe and sandpipers. Some are much rarer than formerly because of the destruction of their habitat. They have long legs and long, slender bills, straight in some species, slightly upturned in others. Of the two European species, the black-tailed godwit has a straight bill. It can be distinguished in flight by a broad white wing-bar and a white tail with a black band. The other European species, the bar-tailed godwit, has no wing bar and its tail is white with

The black-tailed godwit lives in Europe and Asia and migrates to Africa, south-east Asia and Australia. The bar-tailed godwit is a more northern species but migrates south in winter, occasionally reaching South Africa, Australia and New Zealand. Both these birds breed occasionally in Britain. The Hudsonian godwit lives in North America and migrates to South America, sometimes going as far south as the Falkland Islands. The marbled godwit is the most sedentary, breeding in North and Central America, but not migrating any farther south.

agriculture and building, so the numbers of black-tailed godwits have declined. In Britain their numbers fell drastically until the mid-19th century when they became extinct, but they now breed again in small numbers. In Central Europe there has also been a decrease but the bird has spread northwards to Finland in recent years and in the first half of this century its numbers increased in Holland, where it nested in the grass fields of reclaimed polders. The bar-tailed godwit is a coastal species, and in its isolated northern home it seems to be suffering less from man's activities.

Outside the breeding season godwits live in flocks, sometimes twittering to each other

△ *Intruders! A godwit takes to the air to draw attention from the nest.*

Arthur Christiansen

△ *A pause for preening while fishing in the shallows.*

G Rüppell

close black bars. Its bill is slightly upturned. On the ground, distinction is difficult. In summer both have chestnut plumage on head and breast, although the female bar-tailed godwit is much duller than the male. The winter plumage of both species is more like that of a curlew. In North America, the marbled godwit also has a curlew-like plumage and is the same size as a curlew. Its bill is slightly upturned. The Hudsonian godwit looks very dark from a distance. The underparts are brown and the upperparts almost black.

Reduced ranges

Godwits are becoming rare in many parts of their ranges. The marbled godwit has declined as its breeding haunts on the plains and prairies have been cultivated. In 1832, Audubon found flocks of many thousands in Florida, but AC Bent, writing in 1927, said that the species was then rare in Florida. The huge flocks migrating down from New England had been reduced to a few stragglers. The Hudsonian godwit is now very rare.

The black-tailed godwit nests in wetlands; bogs, moors and water meadows, or on dunes, and winters in marshes and estuaries. As wet country is progressively drained for

on the ground or calling in flight, but the winter flocks are not as noisy as the groups of godwits on the breeding grounds, where there is a babble of different calls. Flocks of bar-tailed godwits can often be seen gambolling in the air, especially at the end of the breeding season. Each bird dives and soars, twisting about, wheeling and turning, in contrast with the neat, military manoeuvres usually executed by flocks of waders.

Chasing the waves

Inland, godwits feed on insects and their larvae and worms which they dig out of the soil with their bills or seek among vegetation or mud in shallow water. From water, small fish, tadpoles and water snails are taken, from land, grasshoppers and dragonflies. Along the shore, godwits search for food at the tideline. As a wave recedes, the flock rushes down the beach behind it, snapping up small crustaceans, marine worms and molluscs that have been exposed by the wave's action. Then, as the next wave rolls in, the flock retreats, opening their wings and sprinting pell-mell if the wave is too quick for them. If there is time they probe for lugworms buried deep in the sand, and sometimes they will bury head and neck as well as bill, in order to grapple them.

fly about calling and the male also displays on the ground, strutting around the female with tail spread. The black-tailed godwit, however, indulges in fewer aerobatics than the bar-tailed.

Godwits do not nest in colonies but their nests are usually grouped together. The nest is in a hollow made by pressing down grass and is liberally lined with dead grass and bents. Both parents incubate 5 bluish-grey eggs but the male appears to take the greatest share of incubation. The eggs hatch in 24 days and the chicks leave the nest shortly after their down has dried. They are cared for by both parents until they can fend for themselves.

and, at least formerly, they were present in large numbers for the taking. Shooting them was ludicrously easy because a flock will continually circle back over a fallen companion. Audubon found that the temptation to shoot more than were needed for specimens and food was often very great.

Occasionally a godwit is found to be as foolhardy as a dotterel (p. 798). Bent once found a godwit's nest and decided to go back ½ mile to collect his camera. (One did not carry the cumbersome cameras of 1906 around without good reason.) He got within 15 ft and set up the camera on its tripod and exposed a plate. Then he moved up to 10 ft and repeated the manoeuvre. Emboldened,

Pamela Harrison

△ *If one of the flock falls, the rest will circle overhead, presenting an irresistible target for hunters. No wonder it is becoming a rare bird.*

Aerobatic mating display
In the breeding season the male godwit performs a spectacular display flight. He flies up steeply on rapidly beating wings uttering a 3-syllable call. At a height of about 200 ft the wingbeats slow down and the call changes to the musical call that has led to the Dutch name of *grutto* for the godwit. During this phase of the display flight, the godwit rolls from side to side with his tail spread. He may continue like this for a mile before closing his wings and tail and nose-diving at speed. About 50 ft clear of the ground he spreads his wings and sideslips about, finally landing with wings held vertically. At other times male and female

Feigning injury
Like many seabirds, godwits fly out as an intruder approaches, circling and calling. It is then very difficult to find the eggs or young and the parents make it more difficult by feigning injury, luring a would-be predator away from the defenceless brood. The adults fall prey to hawks unless they can outmanoeuvre them and dive to cover or into the water.

Foolishly tame

Apart from their nesting grounds being destroyed, godwits have suffered from hunting. They are large enough to make a good meal

he crept up to 5 ft then to 3 ft, and, hardly daring to breathe and moving slowly, climbed under the cloth. In the end he decided to photograph the eggs and found that his caution had been wasted: he had to lift the godwit off its nest.

class	**Aves**
order	**Charadriiformes**
family	**Scolopacidae**
genus & species	***Limosa fedoa*** *marbled godwit*
	L. haemastica *Hudsonian godwit*
	L. lapponica *bar-tailed godwit*
	L. limosa *black-tailed godwit*

A potential stowaway; weighing in at ⅙ oz. the diminutive goldcrest has learnt to take advantage of its size. It has even been seen stealing a ride on the back of a migrating owl.

Goldcrest

*Once known as the gold-crested wren, this is the smallest British bird, but is not related to the wren, which is often thought to be the smallest native bird in Britain. The goldcrest, however, weighs only ⅙ oz, half the weight of a wren; by comparison, a house sparrow weighs 1 oz. Other names for the goldcrest are golden-crested regulus and golden-crowned kinglet. The name kinglet is applied to the other four members of the same genus, **Regulus**, all of which have brilliantly coloured patches on their heads. They belong to the warbler family. Of the two in the New World, the American golden-crowned kinglet probably belongs to the same species as the European goldcrest.*

The different names of the goldcrest refer to the bright golden-yellow patch, edged with black, in the centre of the crown. This can be seen only at close quarters, otherwise a goldcrest is a most inconspicuous bird, dull green with whitish underparts. In form it is much like a tit with a rounded body and short, pointed bill. The goldcrest breeds from the British Isles to Japan. It is found over most of Europe except the north of Scandinavia, most of Spain, Italy and southeastern Europe. In recent years the goldcrest has increased in many places because of the spread of conifer plantations.

Small birds similar to the goldcrest can be seen occasionally in the winter in Britain. These are firecrests that live in Europe, North Africa and many parts of North America. They can be distinguished from goldcrests by black stripes on the head. Close inspection shows that the crown is more orange than that of the goldcrest.

Found in evergreens

Goldcrests are fairly tame and can be watched from close quarters flitting about rapidly from tree to tree. Outside the breeding season they live in small groups, sometimes mixing with tits and creepers. The first thing that attracts one's attention to them is their thin, shrill calls of 'zee-zee-zee', which are so high-pitched that they can only just be heard. Then they can be seen flying from trees or through foliage in a straight line with a titlike flight. They are usually found in evergreens, especially outside the breeding season. Goldcrests can be readily recognised by their habit of hovering hummingbird-like in front of foliage. They will hang steadily for 2–3 seconds while searching for food before moving on.

Some goldcrests migrate in the autumn. In the British Isles there is a general southerly movement and goldcrests of the continental race, slightly paler than British goldcrests, appear on the eastern coasts of Britain and spread inland. Before the next breeding season the movement is reversed.

Insect eaters

The continual flitting from tree to tree is in search of food. Goldcrests are insect-eaters and pick small insects, including beetles, aphids and flies, together with their eggs and larvae, from bark and foliage, often hovering, or hanging upside down like tits in the process. In the winter when insects are scarce, goldcrests will eat small seeds and buds.

Life on a swing

Breeding begins in April or May and two broods are raised by the end of the summer. The goldcrest's song is as thin and feeble as its call. This is characteristic of all kinglets except the ruby-crowned kinglet. Perhaps compensating for the weakness of the song, the males display their colourful crowns at rivals and prospective mates. The crown can be spread sideways and vibrated to make it conspicuous.

The nest is usually built in the foliage of an evergreen but has been found in ivy-covered trunks or, extremely rarely, in holes in trees. The usual nest is a cup of moss with a little grass, bound together by spiders' webs and lined with feathers. It is 3 in. across and 3 in. deep, and one can but admire the skill of the goldcrest, only 3½ in. long itself, that collects such a large amount of material and manages to form it into a nest that is slung like a hammock from the twigs and needles. It seems such a precarious position for a nest, as it is thrown to and fro by the slightest wind. The foliage, however, protects it, and squirrels are probably the only enemies that can climb out to it.

Goldcrests lay 7–10 eggs, sometimes as many as 13, each about ½ in. long—an awe-inspiring productivity. The eggs are incubated by the female alone, for about 16 days. Both parents feed the young, which fledge in about 3 weeks. Goldcrest populations are severely hit by hard winters, but with each pair producing a possible score or more offspring in one season, their numbers soon recover.

Hitch-hiker

Throughout Europe there are legends of the antagonism between the eagle and the wren, often about their vying to be king of the birds. The most familiar story is that of the competition to see which bird could fly highest. Surprisingly the diminutive wren won, but it was by means of a trick. It hid among the eagle's feathers and when the latter had flown as high as it could the wren emerged and flew a little bit higher, so becoming king of the birds. It has been suggested that the bird concerned was really the goldcrest, whose golden circle of feathers has led to its being given a name such as kinglet in several languages. In his book *The folklore of birds*, the Rev EA Armstrong dismisses this, pointing out that in many other languages the wren's name implies kingship, and that it would be surprising that the legend would have been transferred from one bird to another without any traces in the folklore of Europe. His view is that traditionally it is the Jenny wren that is the king of birds. But there is just one piece of evidence: a migrating short-eared owl was once found carrying a goldcrest on its back.

class	**Aves**
order	**Passeriformes**
family	**Muscicapidae**
genus & species	***Regulus regulus*** *goldcrest* ***R. ignicapillus*** *firecrest* ***R. calendula*** *ruby-crowned kinglet others*

Golden eagle

Often dubbed the 'King of Birds', only kings could use golden eagles for hawking in medieval Europe. Both flight and stance are majestic; golden eagles measure up to 36 in. long, females being larger than males. The plumage is dark, chocolate brown, tinged with yellow on the head. Young birds have white tails, with a broad, dark band across the base, and white on the undersides of the wings. In flight the wings appear broad with the primaries separated and curving upwards. From a distance, when size is difficult to judge, it is quite easy to confuse golden eagles and buzzards.

Golden eagles are found right across the northern hemisphere. In North America they range from Alaska to Mexico, mainly on the western side of the continent, but they range across Canada, between Hudson's Bay and the Great Lakes, to Nova Scotia. In the eastern hemisphere golden eagles range from northern Britain, Norway and Spain to Kamchatka and Japan. They are found over most of Asia north of the Himalayas, but in Europe they are found in Scandinavia, Scotland, northern Ireland and in parts of the south, including Spain, Greece and the Balkans, Italy and the central mountain ranges of Europe. In Africa they are confined to Tunisia, Algeria and Morocco.

Lord of vast territories

The home of the golden eagle is in open mountainous country, occasionally in forests or plains, but in these latter places it is usually replaced by the imperial eagle. In Scotland the golden eagles increased after the 1940s. In the Highlands numbers are now fairly steady and eagles have spread into the lowlands and northern England. Each pair has a vast home range, up to 16 sq. miles, where they live all the year round. They do not necessarily hunt over all this range, and, in the Highlands at least, it appears that there is a surplus of food within the range of each pair. So the range size, and consequently the number of eagle pairs in an area is not determined by the food supply. In a 10-year study of some golden eagles in Scotland it was found that if the main source of food for a pair failed, as after myxomatosis, the eagles survived without difficulty.

The range is not defended so vigorously as is the territory of a garden songbird such as a robin or blackbird. Occasional squabbles break out but the limits of a range are usually demonstrated by a spectacular display flight following the usual hawk pattern. All through the year golden eagles can be seen, either singly or in pairs, flying upwards in a spiral then diving on half-closed wings, or flying up and down as if on a switchback. Other eagles especially juveniles are allowed into the home range and they may wander some distance. Golden eagles in Ireland have been found with the remains of the Scottish mountain hare by their eyries.

Carl Zwikl: Bavaria

△ *Talons and beak at the ready, the lord of the open mountain ranges prepares to pounce. This majestic bird is so confident of its power that it has been known to attack, and damage, an aeroplane.*
▽ *An outcrop on a craggy rock above vast hunting grounds is an appropriate setting for an eyrie.*

JH Sears

King of the crags

Majestic yet swift in flight, lord over vast territories, and faithful to his mate until death, the golden eagle is truly a monarch of the bird kingdom.

◁ *Power in action; the female, larger than the male, can have a wingspan of 8 ft. The nest of heather will be used by the couple year after year until one of them dies, when the survivor will search for a new mate.*

▽ *A watchful parent supervises the educational play of its offspring. The beak, strengthened by playing with twigs, will soon be tearing at carcases.*

Arthur Brook

Eric Hosking

Other places may be communal hunting grounds. The abundance of food within the range and the tolerance towards trespassers helps in winter when food may be abundant in one place but scarce elsewhere.

Sheep-slaughter myth

The food of golden eagles varies throughout its range. It consists mainly of small animals, predominantly mammals, together with birds, snakes, and rarely fish. A large amount of carrion is also eaten. In a survey made in the Highlands, mountain hares, rabbits, grouse and ptarmigan made up the bulk of the golden eagles' diet. They also ate foxes, stoats, pigeons, pipits, and voles

in small numbers. In America snakes and even tortoises are taken. On rare occasions lambs or deer calves were killed but these were usually eaten as carrion.

Golden eagles hunt by flying low over the ground or by perching on a favoured tree or rock, then swooping down at an incredible speed to seize their prey and kill it. They have been seen beating hares from cover and have been known to employ subtle stratagems. In the Hebrides a pair of golden eagles were seen to co-operate in capturing a lamb. One distracted the ewe's attention while the other approached to seize the lamb. They have also been seen apparently trying to drive deer over cliffs.

Small well-tended family

In the breeding season the male and female indulge in the same display flights as are used for advertising their home range. The male also chases the female swooping or circling over her, while she may roll on to her back. They mate for life, but if one eagle is killed its mate finds a new partner at the next breeding season, and if both die the range does not stay vacant for long.

The same nest is used from year to year. In Scotland it is usually on a cliff edge, but may be on a tree or on the ground. In North America trees are used more often. The nest is built of sticks taken from trees, or in open country of sprigs of heather. Bracken and ferns are also used. Both birds bring material and pieces are added throughout the breeding season. Two eggs, white flecked with brown or grey, are laid and incubated by the female for about 40 days. The male only occasionally feeds his mate while she is incubating, but he brings most of the food needed by the chicks. At first the chicks, clad in down, are almost helpless and the parents have to feed them. Later they become stronger and crawl about the nest playing with sticks and learn to tear carcasses and feed themselves. They leave the nest after about 10 weeks and may not immediately fly but remain perched on a ledge waiting for their parents.

threatened by afforestation destroying their usual open habitats.

Dangerous to whom?

There are very few authentic cases of golden eagles attacking humans. Very rarely small children are attacked, but stories of children being found unhurt in eyries are all untrue because eagles habitually kill their prey before bearing it away. Golden eagles are tolerant of intruders at their nests, especially as compared with many much smaller birds such as drongos (p. 806). In 1968 however, a helicopter flying over Uzbekistan was attacked by two golden eagles which dive-bombed, then chased it. This is not an isolated instance. Once, golden eagles were controlled in Texas by shooting them from a plane. It was necessary to fly very close to the eagles. Sometimes the tables were turned and one eagle dived at a plane and flew right into it, tearing large holes in the aircraft.

class	Aves
order	Falconiformes
family	Accipitridae
genus & species	*Aquila chrysaetos*

A Himalayan golden eagle, the rarest in the world. This 20lb specimen was once used by Khirghity tribesmen to hunt wolves that threatened their flocks.

Keystone

Pesticides spell danger

Golden eagles are often killed because of the harm, real or imagined, that they do to livestock, but it is only in the last few years that they have really faced extinction. In the Scottish Highlands the percentage of pairs successfully rearing young fell from 72% up to 1960 to 29% in the next three years. This was a quite remarkable drop and was almost certainly due to DDT poisoning and the more toxic dieldrin. Most of this was from sheep carcasses and was absorbed when the sheep were dipped to control insect pests. The poisons rendered the eagles infertile. In 1966 dieldrin for sheep was banned and eagle populations recovered. Now they are

Golden eagle
(Aquila chrysaetos)

Nature's steam shovel with no reverse gears. The golden mole is prodigiously strong and can move a weight over a hundred times its own; but it cannot reverse against the set of its fur. It has to keep following its nose in the dark underground domains.

Barry Driscoll

Golden mole

Golden moles look and behave like true moles but are more nearly related to shrews. It has even been suggested that they are not insectivores but should be placed in a separate order, an idea not favoured by most zoologists. The smallest is 3 in. long, the largest just over 9 in. They have the rounded, cylindrical body of a true mole, with very short legs and the claws on the front feet enlarged and used in digging. They are blind, the eyes being small and covered with hairy skin. The ears are small and hidden in the fur. The muzzle ends in a leathery pad and the nostrils are hidden under a fold of skin. The skin is tough and loose and the fur is thick with a dense, woolly underfur, and it has a metallic sheen which may be yellow, red, green, bronze or violet. There are 20 species of golden moles in Africa south of the Sahara, mainly in southern Africa.

Head used as a bulldozer

Golden moles are usually found where the soil is light and sandy, on plains or in forests, and they are especially common on cultivated ground. They burrow by thrusting their noses downwards into the soil and then bringing the head up. As the soil crumbles it is pushed backwards under the body with the short forelegs, which turn inwards, not outwards as in true moles. Each fore foot has four toes. One has a large curved claw, on the third of its four toes, and there is a slightly smaller one on the second toe. The remaining two are tiny and useless in digging. The hindfeet are used to push the soil farther back. The tunnels are usually just under the surface, the mole pushing its snout through the surface from time to time, wrinkling its snout as if sniffing, then submerging to continue its tunnelling. As a rule the tunnels are used only once. In very loose soil the roof caves in

behind the mole, leaving a furrow. Sometimes a golden mole will drive a shaft several feet down into the earth, possibly for making a nesting chamber.

Turns about by somersaulting

Unlike a true mole's fur, the golden mole's has a set. This means it cannot move against the lie of the fur so to turn around within its burrow a golden mole lowers its head slightly to one side, turns it, and with a quick flip brings the hind quarters over the head. It seems that golden moles are inconvenienced by dry soil in which they shake themselves vigorously. Their fur cannot be wetted and it is never groomed. If the fur gets muddy the mole merely continues burrowing until the mud is rubbed off. Generally, golden moles dig in a leisurely fashion compared with true moles and do not show the same restlessness.

We are told that some species are active by day and others active by night. This may mean that, as in the common European mole, the 24 hours are divided into 3-hourly or 4-hourly alternating periods of feeding and sleep. On the other hand, some may be nocturnal and some diurnal. Some species feed on insects, especially crickets, grasshoppers, locusts and cockroaches, earthworms and snails. Insects are crushed with a few snaps of the cheek teeth, then swallowed quickly. Snails are opened up with the incisors and crushed with the molars.

Earthworms are held in the forefeet and swallowed head-first in one continuous action, without being chewed. Certain legless lizards which burrow in the soil are also eaten.

Golden mole twins

Usually two young are born at a time in a grass-lined cavity in the ground. The Cape golden mole seems to breed in the rainy season, April to July, and the babies are suckled for two or three months, until they cut their first teeth, by which time they are almost mature. There is no information

about enemies, but it is known that one species, DeWinton's golden mole, shams dead when touched – after giving a sharp squeak.

Shivering while asleep

As long as it is awake a golden mole keeps on the move, and it is this exercise which keeps its body temperature normal. If it stays still too long, or if it is unwell, its temperature quickly falls. This suggests that waterlogged soil is probably a natural hazard. One golden mole that died in captivity was found to have contracted pneumonia through being kept in too damp soil. Clearly, sleep would be a hazard for a golden mole without some safeguard, so while it sleeps its muscles keep twitching, to supply at least some of the heat its body would generate when awake and moving about.

Strong-man mole

The South African zoologist, James A Bateman, who has studied golden moles, tells of their strength. A mole *Amblysomus hottentotus* was captured and placed in a glass bowl of the kind used for goldfish. It was filled with soil and over the top was placed a sheet of iron weighted down with a piece of railway metal. At one time the mole escaped by pushing this load of metal with its snout. The metal weighed 21 lb, the mole weighed 2 oz. This helps us to understand how a golden mole can almost literally bore its way through the earth with its nose.

class	**Mammalia**
order	**Insectivora**
family	**Chrysochloridae**
genera & species	***Amblysomus hottentotus*** *African golden mole* ***Cryptochloris wintoni*** *DeWinton's golden mole others.*

Goldfinch

The goldfinch is a very handsome bird, $5\frac{1}{4}$ in. long, named for the golden-yellow bar on each wing. Its back is a tawny brown, its underparts paler. The head is boldly marked with red, white and black. The wings are black with a gold bar and white tips to the flight feathers. The forked tail is black with white tips. The beak is short and conical: a seed-eater's beak.

The young goldfinch lacks the red, white and black of the adult's head. Instead it has lines of spots or streaks on head, back and breast and, except for the golden bar on the wing, looks very like several other closely related finches. One of these is the siskin **Carduelis spinus**, which is about the same size and belongs to the same genus but has more yellow in its plumage. It spends the summer in pine-woods and the winter among the alders along the riverside. Another is the twite **Carduelis flavirostris**, a finch of Scandinavia and northern Britain. The serin **Serinus dermus** is very like the siskin in appearance and habits. It is a European bird that occasionally visits Britain, which also has the lines of dark streaks. In an evolutionary sense all three are less 'grown up' than the gold-finch and show their immaturity in the streaked plumage of the adult.

The goldfinch ranges across Europe into western and southwestern Asia, also North Africa.

A charm of goldfinches

The goldfinch is a showy bird that appears to come from nowhere at certain seasons, especially late summer, when it feeds on the seed heads of herbaceous plants. Except in the breeding season, it goes about in small flocks and attracts attention by its musical twittering and its bold and conspicuous colours seen at close range. When not feeding it perches high up in trees, on the outer twigs, and seen then in silhouette so that its coloured head is obscured, it passes for any one of a half-a-dozen small finches. At night the flocks roost in trees and in winter use oak and beech, especially those in hedges, that are late in shedding their dead leaves. As with other small finches the flight is bounding or undulating.

A flock is usually spoken of as a charm of goldfinches. Originally this was spelled 'chirm', and meant a chorus of sounds and was applied to the chatter of any birds. In recent years it has become restricted to goldfinches. It was this musical twittering that made goldfinches, as well as the related linnets, popular as cage birds.

Diet of seeds

Goldfinches seldom feed on the ground although they may take insects, especially in summer. Their feeding is traditionally associated with the seeding thistle heads but they will visit the seeding heads of other members of the daisy family Compositae. They also take seeds of pine and birch and may visit alders to feed from their catkins, in company with siskins, serins and red-polls. One goldfinch was seen to climb a dandelion stem until it bent over, then nip it, the stem folding at the weakened point. Then she held the top of the stem, as well as the part she was standing on, in her feet and ate the seeds. She did this repeatedly.

Away from the comparative safety of the nest, a young goldfinch faces the world.

Resourceful goldfinch hen

The breeding season begins early in May. The male flashes his golden wing bars at the female, as part of his courtship display, while swaying from side to side. The nest of interwoven roots, bents, wool, moss and lichens, lined with thistledown and wool, is built by the hen, usually well out on a branch but sometimes in a hedge. There have been a number of instances of goldfinches untying the strings of labels used on fruit bushes and weaving the strings into the nests. The 5–6 eggs are bluish white with red spots and streaks, each nearly $\frac{3}{4}$ in. by $\frac{1}{2}$ in. The hen alone incubates for 12–13 days, fed by the cock, but both parents feed the chicks by regurgitation for another 12–13 days. There are sometimes 3 broods a year.

An agility at performing tricks with string made the goldfinch a popular cage bird in the past.

Hauling in the lines

The note included above under breeding behaviour, about goldfinches untying the strings of labels, may appear remarkable, but this is not beyond their known abilities. We are used to stories of tits pulling up strings of nuts to a perch in order to eat but for centuries, according to Dr WH Thorpe, the eminent authority on animal behaviour, goldfinches have been kept in special cages so people could watch what they do. In the 16th century the gold-finch was called the draw-water or its equivalent in several European languages. These captive goldfinches were in cages so designed that to survive they had to do precisely this. On one side was a little cart containing seed and this was held by a string. The goldfinch had to pull the string with its beak, hold the loop with one foot, then pull in another loop with the beak, hold that, and so on until it could take the seeds. Another string held a thimble of water. To drink, the bird had to draw this up in the same way.

Canaries and other captive birds have been seen to do similar things, and the performances are not confined to cage birds. In 1957, it was reported from Norway and Sweden that hooded crows were stealing fish and bait from fishermen's lines set through holes in the ice. A crow would take the line in its beak and walk backwards away from the hole. Then it would walk forward again, carefully treading on the line to stop it slipping back. It would repeat this until the fish or the bait was drawn to the edge of the ice, when it would seize it.

class	Aves
order	Passeriformes
family	Fringillidae
genus & species	*Carduelis carduelis*

A 'celestial' goldfish: his eyes are turned for ever towards the heavens.

▷ *An aquarium: a fish society in miniature.*

Goldfish

Goldfish are, in fact, a domesticated form of a wild carp native to China. The wild ancestral form is a very ordinary fish, sometimes used as food, green and brown in colour but occasionally throwing up red or red-gold individuals. These were collected and cultivated by the Chinese as far back as 960 AD and by the period 1173–1240 goldfish were being kept as pets in earthenware bowls and ornamental ponds. They were introduced into Japan in 1500 but reached Europe nearly two centuries later. There is reason to believe that the first reached England in 1692 on a ship that left Macao in 1691. From then on, goldfish reached France in 1750, the Netherlands in 1753 or 1754, Germany in 1780 and in Russia there were goldfish in bowls in Prince Potemkin's Winter Garden in 1791. Goldfish did not reach the United States apparently until 1859.

The relationships of the goldfish have been variously stated by experts. That its ancestor is the crucian carp which is also known as the Prussian carp when it is lean, is one variation. The opinion now seems to be that the goldfish **Carassius auratus** is Asiatic, and that the Prussian carp **C. auratus gibelio,** which is greyish-yellow to silver-grey, is a European subspecies. The crucian carp

of Europe is a separate species **C. carassius.**

Usually regarded as a small fish, the goldfish can weigh up to 10 lb, although those bred as ornamentals are usually only a few inches long. There are two types of fancy goldfish, the scaled and the 'scaleless', the latter having scales that are transparent and hard to see. At first the scaled varieties are uncoloured, that is smoky or like tarnished silver, then black begins to show and later changes to red or white. The scaleless varieties do not have the metallic sheen of the others but show more delicate colours, such as lavender and blue. They are white at first, sprinkled with dark specks, and quickly gain their permanent colours. The shubunkin is a familiar example of the 'scaleless' type, blue tinged with red and mottled with yellow, red and dark brown, or in some combination of these colours.

Golden mudlarks

The life of the wild goldfish is no more eventful than that of the domesticated varieties. The natural food includes animal and plant, the first including water fleas, freshwater shrimps *Gammarus*, gnat larvae and worms (especially *Tubifex*). Among the water fleas are Cyclops and *Daphnia* (see p. 747), the latter so familiarly known to aquarists as a food for aquarium fishes that the name is anglicized, usually to daphney. The plant food includes duckweed and, in the aquarium the small green algae that tend to coat the wall of the aquarium. This

is augmented by mouthfuls of mud, the fish chewing this over by churning movements of the jaws. The inedible matter is spat out and the fragments of dead plant and animal matter swallowed. By what extraordinary means the two are sorted is not fully understood.

Pearly king

Male and female become recognizable at the breeding season because the female is then swollen with eggs while the male develops tubercles known as pearl organs on the gill covers and pectoral fins. These are difficult to see without viewing the fish from a certain angle. The female lays 500–1 000 eggs, each $\frac{1}{16}$ in. diameter, between May and August, which are fertilised after they have been laid, the male following the female around all the time she is spawning. The eggs stick to the water plants. They hatch in 8–9 days when the temperature is 16–18°C/60–65°F, in 5–7 days at 21–24°C/70–75°F. The larvae, $\frac{1}{5}$ in. long and tadpole-like in shape, hang on to the water plants for the next 48 hours, by which time the yolk sac is emptied, the fins have grown and the baby goldfish are able to feed on infusorians (microscopic protozoa). When 18 days old they will be 1 in. long and will feed on water fleas, especially 'daphney'. In the aquarium they are usually given packaged foods, especially ants' 'eggs'.

Danger of infancy

Pet goldfish can be long-lived, up to 25 years having been recorded, but life for the wild form is more precarious. The enemies are predatory fishes, fish-eating birds such

A beautiful freak of nature bred by man, a veiltail would never survive outside the artificial world of the aquarium.

as herons and kingfishers, as well as aquatic mammals. The losses from these may represent perhaps 5–10% of the adult population. The real wastage takes place in the early stages of life, especially among the baby fishes, where the death-rate is 70–80% during the first 6 months to a year. The enemies then are many both for the wild stock and for goldfish in ornamental ponds.

Wherever in this encyclopedia the enemies of freshwater fishes are considered they must include much the same as those now to be listed for the baby goldfish. What follows here can, therefore, serve as a standard for the general run of freshwater fishes, with the advantage that those who keep goldfish in ornamental ponds can know who their enemies are. The freshwater hydra, leeches, pond skaters or water striders, water scorpions and water boatmen or backswimmers, as well as a variety of beetles are the main enemies, together with dragonfly larvae. On top of these there are bacterial and fungal diseases. The enemies that do the most damage are probably the various beetles, the whirligig, the great diving and the great silver beetles. The larvae and the adults of the first two attack

baby fishes, and so do the larvae of the third. The larva of the great diving beetle *Dytiscus* has been called the water tiger, the larva of the great silver beetle *Hydrophilus* is called the spearmouth by American aquarists. Both names are justified.

Beautiful freaks

The more fancy breeds of goldfish are freaks, no matter how attractive some of them may look. To recite their names is enough to make this point: veiltail, eggfish, telescope, calico, celestial, lionhead, tumbler, comet or meteor and pearl scale. There are also the water bubble eye, blue fish, brown fish, brocade, pompon and fantail and many others. Some breeds are monstrosities rather than freaks. The veiltail with long curtain-like tailfins, doubled in number, is a reasonable freak. The eggfish has a rounded body and has lost its dorsal fin. The telescope has large bulging eyes which may, rarely, be tubular. The lionhead has not only lost its dorsal fin and grown a rounded body but its swollen head is covered with rounded bumps and looks more like a raspberry.

Students of fishes have sometimes noted

that certain freaks arise more or less frequently in nature. Under domestication natural mutants or freaks, or monstrosities that appear are selected and bred to produce new strains. In goldfish the most frequent are the doubling of the tail fin or of the anal fin, the loss of the dorsal fin, and eyeballs that are outside the sockets. Where goldfish have gone wild, however, as they have in southern France, Portugal, Mauritius and the United States, the descendants of the more normal goldfish quickly revert to the wild form, in colour and in shape. Under these conditions the more freakish varieties are at a disadvantage and soon are eliminated—which is what happens to the freaks in any wild species.

class	**Osteichthyes**
order	**Cypriniformes**
family	**Cyprinidae**
genus & species	***Carassius auratus***

Male, with mate and family below.

All three are part of a Prague zoo study.

Hard going even for Good King Wenceslas; goral survive by digging for acorns, eating branches.

Goral

Like its relatives the serow, chamois and Rocky Mountain goat, the goral is a goat-antelope well adapted to a life on mountains. The male goral stands up to 2½ ft at the shoulder — slightly larger than the female — and weighs 50 − 70 lb. The legs are long and stout, adapted for climbing and jumping, the coat usually long and shaggy with a short woolly undercoat and long coarse guard hairs, and the 6in. horns curve backwards. There are three species. The grey goral's coat is shaggy, grey to grey-brown, often grizzled with black, and there is a white throat patch. The brown goral has a short brown coat with white patches on throat and chest. The red goral has a long shaggy coat, bright fox-red with no throat or chest patches. It is smaller than the other two and has shorter ears. The grey goral ranges from northern Burma and Kashmir through the mountain systems of western and northern China to Korea and the Sikhote Alin region of eastern Siberia. The brown goral is known from a single specimen from the dry country of the upper Brahmaputra, in southeastern Tibet. The red goral lives in the mountains of northern Burma and Assam.

Inaccessible habitats

Goral occupy a variety of habitats in different parts of their range. In Szechwan the grey goral lives at altitudes of 5 000 − 8 500 ft in the steep, arid, often almost vertical gorges of the big rivers (Yangtse, Yalung, Mekong). The vegetation consists of short stubbly grass and thornbushes such as junipers, barberry and rose. Farther up, at 10 000 − 13 500 ft, it lives in the moist valleys of small mountain torrents, very craggy but still with thick vegetation, from thick bush to forest. In the northern part of its range, in the Sikhote Alin, it lives on the precipitous coastal cliffs, going down to sea level; the vegetation here consists of stunted oaks, stone-pines, and shrubby forms of maple and dwarf juniper, while at the top are oak forests. Inland in the same region the goral lives at altitudes of up to 3 500 ft on rubble-covered slopes interlaced with small wooded grasslands and deciduous forests.

Goral are found in small, isolated pockets, and it is difficult to see how inbreeding, with the deterioration that follows it, is avoided, since these animals do not move about much. The red goral is found at higher altitudes than the grey. It seldom comes much below 8 000 ft and ranges in summer above the tree-line, which is around 12 000 ft.

Eating whatever is to hand

In summer, goral live by grazing, but in autumn they go into more forested regions and eat mainly leaves, also acorns, which they dig out of the snow with their snouts. In February and March, when the snowfall is greatest, they eat mainly branches. In winter the animals are constantly up to their bellies in snow, and have to jump to move about. The ewes and juveniles live in groups of 2 − 12, but the adult males are solitary for most of the year. Goral are active mainly in the morning and evening. After the morning feed they go down into the valley to drink, then lie out in the sun on a ledge, motionless, with the feet tucked under and the head stretched out in front.

the high mountains nearby. In 1913 in the Mishmi Hills, just over the border in Assam, some of these red goral were shot. In March or April, 1922, HL Cooper was shooting in the Mishmi Hills and shot a takin at a salt lick. Grazing on a steep slope above the salt lick were some bright red goral, and the Mishmi tribesmen with him killed four or five of them for meat. In 1931, the Earl of Cranbrook shot a red goral in the Adung valley, on the extreme upper Irrawaddy in northern Burma, and presented it to the British Museum.

These facts did not come together to form a coherent picture until 1960, when Mr Cooper sent a rug from his home in Guernsey to the British Museum for identification. This was made from the skins of three of the animals shot in 1922. RW Hayman, at that time in the Mammal Section, recognised them as belonging to the same species as the Earl of Cranbrook's, and at once all the pieces of the jigsaw fell into place. Mr Hayman published a description of the species.

In a later paper, he described the skull of one of Mr Cooper's goral, sent over by the Bombay Natural History Society, and established that there were differences in the skulls too. At the same time, he re-examined the type specimen of the brown goral, described by Pocock as long ago as 1914 and named after Lt-Col Bailey, and was able to show that this, too, was a separate species and not just a race of the common species, as had been previously thought. Unfortunately, no second specimen of the brown goral is known. In January, 1964, a female red goral was captured near Lashio, in the northern Shan States of Burma, and sent to the Rangoon zoo where it still lives. It is a very agile animal; on one occasion it jumped the 6ft barrier of its enclosure from a standstill! It sleeps on the top of its hut, 5½ ft above the ground.

class	**Mammalia**
order	**Artiodactyla**
family	**Bovidae**
genus & species	***Nemorhaedus baileyi*** brown goral ***N. cranbrooki*** red goral ***N. goral*** grey goral

Grey goral. These rare goat-antelope are being bred in a state wildlife park in the western Himalayas.

Dependent calves

The rams join the groups of ewes in the middle or end of September and go back to their solitary life after mating in the first half of November. The calves are born in early May in Szechwan, but not until June in the Sikhote Alin. They lie hidden among rocks while the ewes graze nearby. Usually there is only one at a birth; twins are rare, triplets rarer. They are suckled until late autumn, but stay with their mothers until the following spring. Goral may live as much as 15 years.

Enemies

In the really steep habitats, the only serious predators are eagles, which take the calves. In the higher, less steep country of the interior of Szechwan, leopards feed on them.

Goral offer poor trophies to the hunter but present a challenge to the sportsman because of the difficulties of their habitat. They are commonly hunted for sport, often with dogs, against which they defend themselves courageously with their horns. They make a hissing sound when frightened.

Species from a rug

Until 1961, only one species of goral was known, although evidence for the other two was already available. In 1863, Edward Blyth reported that the goral of Assam is 'bright rufous'. In 1912 Lt-Col FM Bailey saw people at Sanga Chu Dzong in SE Tibet wearing red fur coats. On being questioned they revealed that the fur came from a type of goral which was plentiful in

A mystery for zoologists: grey goral live in inaccessible places in isolated herds, yet there is no evidence of deterioration caused by inbreeding.

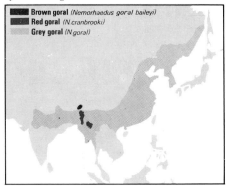

Brown goral *(Nemorhaedus goral baileyi)*
Red goral *(N.cranbrooki)*
Grey goral *(N.goral)*